Christian Principles for Recovery:

A Workbook for the Addicted

and those who want to help!

7 Principles Of Recovery

A Workbook

by

Virgil L. Stokes

Faith Christian Fellowship of Tucson

P.O. Box 89156 • Tucson, AZ 85752

E-mail: virgil@fcftucson.org • **Web Site:** www.fcftucson.org

TABLE OF CONTENTS

SEVEN PRINCIPLES OF RECOVERY

Webster says recovery is, (a) a regaining of something lost or stolen, (b) a return to health, consciousness, etc., (c) a regaining of balance, control, composure, etc."
[1]

ROMANS 12:2
"Don't copy the behavior and customs of this world, but let God transform you into a new person by changing the way you think. Then you will know what God wants you to do..."

(New Living Translation)

This workbook is specifically intended for the individual who thinks he may have a problem with addiction. It is designed to give information, encouragement, and specific instruction to assist in the process of diagnosis and recovery. Hopefully, the same material will be helpful to those who are attempting to design a program helpful to the addict.

The entire workbook will be focused on seven principles. We want to emphasize principles, not programs. A principle is a piece of practical truth which may be applied in different settings with the same results. The format will be simple. Each principle will be defined, then discussed. The discussion will be followed by a series of practical applications and exercises. These will consist of a variety of specific instructions and activities for the person in recovery.

In order to understand the aim of this section, it is necessary to understand what we mean by recovery. "Recovery" is the process of healing and restoration which brings an individual to wholeness. This includes physical and mental healing, repairing of damaged relationships, and a new intimacy with the Creator.

When we come to Christ we are all recovering from something. Exposure to the world and its ways leaves scars on the best of us. The whole of the Christian life is in some sense a recovery process. In **ROMANS 12:2** the Apostle Paul tells us that we must be transformed by the renewing of our minds or we will, even as believers, be conformed to this world and fall short of the perfect will of God. The word "renewing" means to make new again. Strong's Exhaustive Concordance uses the term "renovation." The picture is one of a remodeling job on an old house. We systematically go through the rooms of our mind, dust off the contents, and one piece at a time we throw away the dead, dark, and ungodly thoughts of our old life and replace them with the life and light of the Word of God.[1]

The addict has the same job as every Christian. He must grow in faith while being transformed by the renewing of his mind. Because he is an addict, he has some old ways of thinking that are common to most addicts and not so common to other people. At the same time, he also has many of the same issues as everyone else. Everyone is self-centered. Greed, lust, bitterness! We all fight the same foes to one degree or another. The problem for the addict

---

1   *Webster's New World Dictionary*, **Second College Edition (Simon & Schuster, New York, 1984). Pg. 1188.**

is in helping him to stay straight long enough to get established in God. If he should begin to use again there is no guarantee he can make it back. The Lord told me years ago that my counseling ministry was simply designed to keep people alive long enough for Him to get a firm foothold in their lives. This is doubly true of the addict.

The following principles are valid for everyone. For the addict they are essential, not just to Christian living, but to living at all. It is genuinely a matter of life and death.

DEFLATION

Webster tells us that "deflate" means to collapse by letting out air or gas, or to make smaller or less important. This is a great description of what the addict needs. He is inflated in his own mind. The Bible refers to pride as being "puffed up" **(1 CORINTHIANS 4:19)**. Pride is a bar to recovery. It prevents the process from ever beginning.

1 CORINTHIANS 4:19
But I will come to you shortly, if the Lord wills, and I will know, not the word of those who are puffed up, but the power.

(New King James)

But I'll be there sooner than you think, God willing, and then we'll see if they're full of anything but hot air.

(Message Bible)

Pride says to the addict, "It can't happen to you. You're unique." Then it says, "You can't ask for help. You would be humiliated." In the face of good advice pride replies, "I'll do it my way." It ultimately says, "It might work for others, but it won't work for you. You're the first person too bad for God to help."

The process of deflating the addict must come on three levels.

1. Admission: He must first admit he has a problem.

2. Desperation: He must then be able to admit that he cannot help himself, that the problem has him.

3. Willingness: Finally, he must become willing to ask another for help and then do what he is told. All of these are very difficult for most addicts.

ADMISSION

I have to admit I have a problem before I will expend any effort to solve it.

The first step in the recovery process is the admission that recovery is necessary. I have to admit I have a problem before I will expend any effort to solve it. This is the first place of confrontation between reality and the blindfold called denial. For the average person, this may seem a paper tiger. Can't we simply present a person with the facts and expect him to make a sound decision? In the case of addicts and alcoholics the answer is emphatically, "NO!" Many is the alcoholic who has gone to an early grave rather than admit he couldn't drink successfully.

The ability to ignore or misinterpret mountains of evidence is the first trick in the bag of every addict. The first line of defense is purely pride. The logic seems to be something like, "It is impossible that I am an alcoholic, because I am me. Alcoholics can't control their drinking. I, of course, could if I wanted to, because I am me." All evidence to the contrary, the alcoholic believes he could control his drinking, if only....

Every alcoholic has a set of "if only's" all his own. Some are as simple as "if only I wanted to." Others are more complex. "If only my boss would ease up," "if only my wife weren't so bitchy," "if only the Suns would play defense," "if only I could get these bills paid," etc. If you are a drinker or drug user, it would be good for you to examine your "if only's". "If only's" are progressive. That is, as each one proves to be untrue, we change them to suit our ever-descending condition. As each "if only " comes to pass, the addict re-decides. He rationalizes his behavior anew and makes up a new "if only" less restrictive than the last one.

When I was in college, I thought I would quit "if only" it became necessary in order to have a good job. When I had a good job, I said I would quit "if only the job weren't so stressful." When I lost the job, I said I could quit "if only I didn't have the pressure of finding a job." After I found another job I said I would quit "if only it became a problem on the job." The "if only's" just keep adjusting themselves downward to conform to the descending spiral of the life of the alcoholic or addict. If you have left a trail of "if only's" behind you, you are in trouble. Normal people, when confronted with the destructive consequences of their drinking, find it within themselves to quit. The addict finds it easier to blame others and adjust his own expectations of himself to a lower level.

It is important to remember that the addict has allowed his relationship with his drug to become the highest priority in his life. He will do anything to protect that relationship. This includes lying to others and to himself. It also includes doing away with activities, responsibilities, and people that demand he give up his chemical lover. He is willing to change friends, jobs, hobbies, families, and values. At each step of the process he is able to convince himself he is doing the right thing, the noble thing, or the only thing. He is actually simply being an addict. He is doing the drug thing.

The addict is a person who is allowing a chemical to make important decisions for him. He is choosing the chemical over the other priorities in his life. I remember talking for hours to one man who insisted he did not have a problem with alcohol. After all, he only drank beer. He was adamant in his denial. In exploring some of his behaviors, we recalled a Saturday morning when he had promised to take his young sons to the zoo. They awakened him from a beer-induced stupor on the couch to ask if he were ready for their excursion. He yelled an emphatic, "No!" and staggered to the refrigerator for a wake-up belt.

After he described this incident I simply said, "Who was more important that day, your sons or your Budweiser?" The reality of his behavior suddenly struck him. He doubled over with the pain that only truth can

What are your "IF ONLY's..."?

An addict is a person who is allowing a chemical to make important decisions for him.

inflict. If you are making **any** decisions to ignore the needs of important people in your life because you would rather drink or drug, or because you are hung over from drinking or drugging, then you are in serious trouble. A normal person, seeing this behavior, would stop his usage immediately. Why don't you?

Seeing ourselves and our addiction in the clear light of day is the most difficult step in recovery. It is painful to loathe yourself. A clear mirror is to be avoided at all costs. I remember one dear man who flirted with A.A. for years. He would admit to drinking a bit too much. But to abstain entirely? That seemed a little severe. After all, he really wasn't hurting anyone. Finally one evening when he returned from visiting the bars, his wife turned on a tape recorder in the kitchen. The next morning she played for him the sound track of his blacked-out rampage. He heard himself cursing his wife, knocking over furniture, threatening violence, and breaking dishes–all the things his wife had described for years to the deaf ear of denial. He heard and was a broken man, even suicidal in his remorse. Deflation can be painful.

> *The disease of alcoholism has symptoms like any other disease.*

The disease of alcoholism and addiction is actually fairly easy to diagnose. Like any disease it has symptoms. If a person shows several of these symptoms, then we can safely say he has the disease. When a child begins to run a fever, scratch, and have little red bumps, we quickly say "measles." If you wake up with chills, a runny nose, and sneezing, you wouldn't hesitate to say "cold." Why then, when we see symptoms of addiction, are we so determined to say "stress and depression?" Because it is a blow to our pride to admit weakness, and we see addiction as weakness. We don't see a disease process, we see a self-inflicted problem caused by a weak will or a moral malfunction. What is needed is a diagnosis, not an indictment.

For a detailed discussion of the symptoms of addiction, see the companion book, *"God Help Me, I Can't Stop!"*. In order to give you a clear opportunity to diagnose yourself, I want to present a little test. Just mark the questions with a check mark if they describe you.

DIAGNOSE YOURSELF

☐   *1. Is there some particular reason why you are concerned about your drinking or drug use at this time?*

☐   *2. Are you drinking or using more often than you used to?*

☐   *3. Does it take more of your drug to get you high than it used to?*

☐   *4. When you use or drink, has the amount of your intake gone up?*

☐   *5. Do you sometimes have the shakes or other discomfort the next morning?*

☐   *6. Do you consider the possibility of a drink or some other kind of drug in the morning to help you feel better for the day?*

☐ 7. *Are there people who are questioning your drinking or drug use?*

☐ 8. *Have you had arguments with your spouse or other loved ones about your usage?*

☐ 9. *Do close friends say you are acting differently these days, or that you undergo some kind of personality change when you drink or use?*

☐ 10. *Have you changed friends recently?*

☐ 11. *If you have made new friends, does their drinking or drug usage seem similar to your own?*

☐ 12. *Do you choose your friends based on their drug use or their drinking habits?*

☐ 13. *Do you consider the availability of alcohol and drugs when you choose social events to attend?*

☐ 14. *Have you had more than 2 or 3 memory lapses (called blackouts) in the past 90 days?*

☐ 15. *After an evening or other period of intoxication, have you forgotten where you left your car or how you got home?*

☐ 16. *Have you had to call someone the next day to fill you in on what you were doing the night before.*

☐ 17. *Do you sometimes regret things that you may have said or done while you were under the influence of drugs or alcohol?*

☐ 18. *Are you ever embarrassed to the extent that you want to avoid certain people or going back to a place where you may have done some foolish things?*

☐ 19. *Do you drink more than the people you are with or do you ever load up your drinks so others don't notice what you are doing?*

☐ 20. *Do you order or mix doubles for yourself while others are drinking singles?*

☐ 21. *Do you carry an extra supply with you in case the host runs out or the bar closes before you are ready to quit?*

☐ 22. *Have you gotten careless about things that used to be important to you, or have you dropped certain activities from your routine?*

☐ 23. *Is your family complaining that you spend less time with them than you used to?*

☐ 24. *Are you less interested in some of your former hobbies or sports or entertainment sources?*

☐ 25. *Have you had legal problems connected to your usage?*

☐ 26. *Are you reducing outside activities that interfere with your drinking or using?*

☐ 27. *Have you thought about changing jobs or maybe even moving to another part of the country where you could make a clean start without the hassles and disadvantages from the past?*

☐ 28. *Do you ever wonder if some of your problems would be lessened, or go away, if you decided to stop drinking or drugging entirely?*

☐ 29. *Have you ever hidden a bottle or lied about how much you use or drink?*

☐ 30. *Have you ever used money you knew should go to pay other obligations to buy drugs or alcohol?*

☐ 31. *Has your doctor suggested you cut back on your intake for health reasons, or do you have physical problems you suspect are drug-related?*

☐ 32. *Have you ever promised yourself that you would really try to cut down on your drinking or drug use without quitting altogether?*

☐ 33. *Have you tried skipping certain nights of the week, or hours of the day, when you wouldn't drink or use at all?*

☐ 34. *Have you tried switching or rotating brands or types of alcohol or kinds of drugs in order to keep from losing control so much?*

☐ 35. *Have you tried putting someone else in charge of your drinking to help you cut down?*

☐ 36. *Have you ever tried to quit, totally, and not been able to?*

☐ 37. *Have you ever set a date or duration when you would actually try to stop but when the time came you found an excuse to continue to use?*

☐ 38. *Was it difficult for you to make this self-examination, and is this a subject you consider too personal to discuss with others?*

☐ 39. *Do you intentionally avoid discussions about your drinking/drugging or its complications?*

☐ 40. *Do you sometimes have your spouse or other persons intervene for you, or make excuses about your tardiness or other related problems?*

☐ 41. *Are you reading this workbook because you suspect there may be something wrong with you? (Normal people quit immediately if there is any question.)*

If quitting is a problem for you, then you have definitely progressed well down the path to destruction.

You need to read on.

Grading is easy. Count the number of questions you checked. If you checked even one, you should quit drinking now. (You should quit using drugs no matter how many you checked. It is illegal.) You are already in a dangerous area. To continue to drink is to tempt fate. It would be safer to just quit.

If you checked three or more, then you are definitely in trouble. The only question is, what will it take to get you to see yourself and take responsibility for your condition? Remember, if you have crossed the line to addiction, there is no going back. No amount of willpower and resolve can do it for you. Just as willpower can't cure a cold, so it cannot cure addiction. The diabetic cannot will his blood sugar down. He must watch his diet, exercise, and take his medicine. It is his responsibility. Even so, the addict is responsible to take the necessary steps to treat his addiction. If he does not, he will die. Unfortunately, he will inevitably destroy others in the process.

No matter what the problem, it does little good to pretend it does not exist. It is time to do the only sensible and courageous thing: **ADMIT THE OBVIOUS.** To help you in establishing your addiction as a reality in your thinking, you should complete the following questions.

1. Describe the circumstances of your first drink or drug usage. How old were you? How were you affected? How did you feel about it? Did it get you in trouble?

_____

_____

_____

_____

_____

_____

_____

_____

_____

_____

_____

_____

2. List all the legal troubles you have been in. Include every traffic ticket, court appearance, and encounter with the legal system. Can you see any connection between these occurrences and your drinking or drug use?

_____

_____

_____   ***Be Honest!***

_____

_____

_____

_____

_____

_____

_____

_____

_____

_____

_____

_____

3. Make a list of the *4 most important people* in your life. You might include your parents, your spouse, your children, your friends, etc. Beside each name write out how that person is affected by your drinking or using. Have they spoken to you about it? What have they said? Have you ever lied to them because of it? Have you ever failed to keep your word or fulfill your responsibilities to them? Have you ever embarrassed them with your behavior while intoxicated? Have you ever spoken words which were unnecessarily hurtful to those you love?

_____

_____

_____

_____

_____

_____

4. Have you ever been in trouble on the job, or even lost a job, because of your usage? This would include coming to work late because of a hangover or not doing a good job because you were intoxicated. It may include being inattentive because you were hung over or were needing a drink. Make a list of all your jobs. How did your chemical use affect your performance? What was the outcome?

_____

_____

_____

_____

_____

_____

Looking at this figure in #5, are there other ways this money could have been spent which would have been of greater benefit to you or your family?

5. What has your drinking or using cost you financially in the last year? Include the cost of the drug, the cost of vehicle repairs and legal fees, the cost of things purchased foolishly while under the influence, the loss of income on the job, and any medical bills incurred as a result of drug-induced conditions or injuries. Be thorough and honest.

_____

_____

_____

_____

_____

6. What health problems do you have which are attributable to the intake of your drug?

_____

_____

_____

_____

Do you have any other conditions which you suspect may be related to your drinking and drugging?

_____

_____

_____

_____

7. Why are you reading this workbook? Did someone suggest it? Are you secretly wondering if you have a problem? If the answer to either of these last two questions is "yes," then why don't you simply quit? Please write out your response.

_____

_____

_____

_____

_____

Now, read aloud what you have written. Does it make sense? Would you buy this reasoning if you heard it from someone else?

8. Refer back to the 41-question list.

How many did you check? _____

How many did you lie to yourself about? _____

Do these numbers alarm you or do they make you angry? _____

If so, why?

_____

_____

_____

_____

_____

_____

_____

_____

_____

Are you reading this workbook because you suspect there may be something wrong with you?

9. Based on what you have learned so far, write a statement either admitting or denying that you are an addict or an alcoholic. Give reasons for your statements. Write it in a way which would convince someone else if they should read it.

_____

_____

_____

_____

_____

_____

It is necessary to give up hope before you can get any hope.

10. If someone else suggested this workbook to you, find that person or someone else whose opinion you respect, and tell them what you have written in #9. What is their response?

_____

_____

_____

_____

11. In light of your conclusions in #9 and the response of another person in #10, what do you feel you should do now? What would be the right and intelligent thing to do?

_____

_____

_____

_____

_____

The second aspect of deflation is DESPERATION.

DESPERATION

Admission is only the first step in a long process. It cracks the door to the possibility of recovery. But simply acknowledging a problem is insufficient to solve it. The old proverb is "Everybody complains about the weather, but nobody does anything about it." This can be true of an alcoholic if he simply nods his head to say, "Yes, I am addicted to alcohol." It is imperative that the addict become desperate enough to seek help.

My wife and I puzzled for years over this concept. We saw drunk after addict after drunk who would give a head nod, and even a tear to the statement, "You're an alcoholic." Unfortunately, they then walked resolutely to the bar to further prove the statement. God finally helped us to understand that these individuals were not yet hopeless. You see, it is necessary to give up hope before you can get any hope. The alcoholic who admits his problem but doesn't seek help is still suffering under the delusion that there is hope for him somewhere other than sobriety.

The problem is a failure to understand the exact nature of the problem. The addict and alcoholic is in a hopeless mess. When he takes the drug or drink into his body it triggers a physical/psychological/emotional chain of events which inevitably leads him to lose control of his own behavior. It may happen immediately or it may take a while, but it always happens. He keeps getting drunk when he did not intend to do so. His behavior while under the influence and the effects of the drug on his body produce all the untoward side effects we have enumerated above.

This remarkable inability to limit his intake to the level of geniality and social grace is caused by a physical craving for the chemical which is never experienced by those not suffering from addictions. They can literally take it or leave it. This is the crux of my problem: When I drink, I crave more alcohol until I am unconscious. There will never be enough.

This "craving" which results from the intake of the drug would not be a problem if the addict simply remained drug free. Unfortunately, the other horn of his dilemma skewers him at this point. When left without the drug, he finds himself in an emotional state which can only be characterized as distraught. He may be quite anxious, even overtly fearful. He will be irritable with himself, others, and the details of life. Patience is in short supply. He may find his attention span is decreased. He cannot concentrate. Sleep may be difficult. His mental processes run constantly to the bottle or the pill or the needle. He goes to sleep thinking about it. It is the first thought when he wakes. He is obsessed.

I cannot live and drink. Unfortunately, I would rather not live in the condition in which I find myself when sober. All my best efforts to control my drinking fail, and I worsen. My periods of sobriety do nothing to improve my mental state. I am dry and miserable. I am told I have a disease which is incurable. My only hope is to stay sober. Much to my chagrin, living sober is intolerable and it seems I can do nothing about it. No amount of self-effort, no counseling, no change of circumstance can bring quiet to my turmoil. I can either drink and die, or stay sober and wish I were dead. The old-timers in A.A. called it an allergy of the body combined with an obsession of the mind. We are hopeless.

This is, of course, the state of anyone who is in the world without God. **EPHESIANS 2:12** lets us see a glimmer of what God thinks about those who live outside His covenant. They are all without hope, though they may not be aware of it. Absolute hopelessness is exactly where each of us must come

This is not a problem of willpower or character. It is a physiological and chemical reality.

EPHESIANS 2:12
In those days you were living apart from Christ. You were excluded from God's people, Israel, and you did not know the promises God made to them. You lived in this world without God and without hope.

(New Living Translation)

That at that time you were without Christ, being aliens from the commonwealth of Israel and strangers from the covenants of promise, having no hope and without God in this world.

(New King James)

before we can pass on to ultimate and eternal hope in Christ. We must reach the end of our rope before we will let go long enough to take hold of His. Deflation requires that we despair of our personal ability to solve our own problem and change ourselves.

Many who read this far will have already tried any number of methods to control or stop their drinking. I read a few years ago of a famous athlete who had a drug problem which was threatening his lucrative career. He testified to reporters that he was controlling his habit by substituting avid golfing for his addiction. This seemed to work until his playing days ended. Shortly after his retirement his name was in the news again as drug- and alcohol-related behaviors began to haunt his life. When a person is married to an addiction, no mistress can keep him forever. He will always go home to his drug of choice.

Maybe you have tried changing jobs. Or maybe a change of address and companions has been your cure. If you have been dodging the addiction demon very long you have discovered its tenacity. Maybe you have tried to temper the effects of your addiction by "cutting down." You drink only on the weekends. You count your drinks and swear to never exceed your limit. You switch to beer to wine to pills to pot and back to beer again. It works for a day, a week, a month. You may tell others that you have it whipped, but there is that little place in your quietness that keeps whispering, "It's only a matter of time." The next binge comes. There is that awful moment in the morning as the fog lifts. Your insides quiver and fear grips you. You shake it off and try again.

Have you reached a place of desperation? Have you tried to quit and failed? Do you secretly find the prospect of living without getting high to be a depressing proposition? In your innermost self, do you really believe you could quit if you wanted? Take a stab at completing the following.

1. Do you believe you can stop drinking or using permanently as a result of your own willpower? _____

If so, then why don't you do it?

_____

_____

_____

_____

2. Have you ever tried to quit and failed? _____

How many times? _____

Absolute hopelessness is exactly where each of us must come before we can pass on to ultimate and eternal hope in Christ.

Deflation requires that we despair of our personal ability to solve our own problem and change ourselves.

Why did you fail? Be careful not to blame other people. Did they really force you to drink?

_____

_____

_____

_____

_____

_____

_____

3. Have you ever been in counseling or a treatment center because of your drinking or drug use? _____

If so, why are you still using?

_____

_____

_____

_____

4. Are there methods for quitting or controlling your drinking which you haven't tried, but you think might work?

_____

_____

_____

_____

The old-timers in A.A. called it an allergy of the body combined with an obsession of the mind.

We are hopeless!

Are there certain circumstances in your life which you feel are responsible for your inability to quit?

_____

_____

_____

_____

5. What aspects of living sober are most frightening to you? Why are they so intimidating?

_____

_____

_____

_____

_____

_____

_____

WILLINGNESS

Willingness is a necessity. Recovery CANNOT take place without it.

The final aspect of deflation is willingness. The addict must go through the process of admitting he has a problem. He must then come to recognize the hopelessness of his situation. He must be desperate. But the world is full of desperate men. Desperation is insufficient to produce a cure. There must be motivation to action. In the case of the addict/alcoholic there must be a willingness to take all the necessary steps to overcome. He must be willing to put aside his pride and ask for help. He must be willing to submit himself to the advice of others. He must be willing to do things he has never done before and to do them without fully understanding their purpose. He must be willing to entertain ideas which he has derided as ignorant. All these things are foreign to the addict, but willingness is a necessity. Recovery cannot take place without it.

You must be willing to...

WILLINGNESS IS A NECESSITY.

In the beginning of my recovery I had several very wise friends and advisors who gave me instructions which did not make sense. One of the most non-sensical was the admonition to do sit-ups every morning. I was encouraged that I should do the same number, at the same time, in the same location every day. In addition, I was told never to leave my house without making my bed. My protest was simple. What does this have to do with staying sober? The answer was simple also. As an alcoholic/addict, I have a shortage of self-discipline. The only way to develop self-discipline is to discipline myself to regularly do something which I do not want to do. It requires no discipline to do that which I enjoy. It is not self-discipline if someone else forces me to do it. I needed to develop the muscles in my character which enable me to impose sanctions on my own behavior in order to obtain a greater good. I thank God I was willing to follow instructions.

An old friend of mine used to say, "To stay straight, I had to reach the place where I was willing to push a peanut down main street with my nose, during rush hour, buck naked."

Hopefully this method of treatment will not be necessary for you, but you need to be ready. Most who fail, fail over things far less humiliating than the peanut-pushing treatment. Some of these stumbling blocks include a failure to ask for help, an unwillingness to follow orders, and a recoiling at spiritual remedies. Let's look at a few of these.

Asking for help requires a degree of humility which is hard for many addicts. The dynamics of this are difficult to fathom. We are dealing with people who have frequently stolen from their own family and been involved in all kinds of illegal and shameful activities. Many have been incarcerated or in such meager circumstances that they have been reduced to begging for financial help. All have found themselves controlled and defeated by a chemical substance. In spite of every personal humiliation, they often find it tough to ask help from someone who has offered their services and demonstrated their ability to stay sober and clean. Until this reticence is overcome, recovery will be elusive.

I suppose this is an affliction related to the difficulty some have in asking directions when they are lost. Some folks will wander the streets aimlessly for hours rather than admit to a stranger that they cannot find their way. After a bit it becomes quite apparent to anyone who is watching, especially to passengers in the same vehicle, that the driver is lost. The humiliation lies in the refusal to ask for help when it is so readily available. The question is, "What is so hard about asking for help?"

Some don't want to ask for help because they feel they are admitting a weakness. Usually, everyone around them is already aware of their weakness and are puzzled by their stubborn refusal to see the obvious. For others, their pride will not allow them to admit that someone knows more than they. While I may be a genuine expert in my profession or my hobby, I must be willing to admit I am a novice in the sobriety game. The person I need to talk to is a man who knows something about staying sober. It doesn't matter if he is a Ph.D. or a manual laborer. If he is able to stay sober after a life of intoxication, I need his wisdom.

What is so hard about asking for help?

For some of us, our upbringing and life experience has made it difficult to reach out. One person recounted being told by her parents that she was stupid and shouldn't need help. Another individual recounted being raised on the dictum, "You made your bed. Now you sleep in it." With this notion comes the bizarre idea that I can never ask for help to get out of a situation which I caused. That would include most of life's problems. One dear lady reported going to her pastor for assistance and being told, "You have a Bible. Why don't you just pray and get help from God." Wherever you got the message that it is wrong to ask for help, I want to tell you that it is a lie. Don't allow yourself to be cheated out of recovery because someone gave you wrong information. Don't let their mistake become your mistake by taking their false ideas as truth.

For many, having crossed the barrier of asking for help, there is the hurdle of following instructions from another human being. Addicts have a peculiar propensity for rebellion. It seems to be a part of their make-up. All humans come equipped with a rebellious streak. When Adam ate the fruit in the Garden of Eden, he allowed the nature of Satan to come into the human race. We all reflect his rebellious nature to one degree or another. The addict, however, often takes this attribute to a higher level. We just don't like to be told what to do. Unfortunately for those who are determined to do it their own way, the blessings of God, including deliverance, are only available to those who will follow instructions.

Try to remember that your absolute best thinking got you to the condition you are in.

Rebellion manifests itself in many ways, but there are really two general types. There is the obvious rebel who comes with a chip on his shoulder and makes no bones about it. His mantra is, "Who do you think you are, telling me what to do!?" This guy can be rather intimidating. He may be loud and verbally hostile, but at least you know where he stands. Because he is open in his reaction, and because his reaction is often simply a reflex conditioned by a lifetime of rebellion, he can often be helped and corrected after he blows off a little steam.

The more difficult type of rebellion is the "Yes, Massah" shuffle. These folks listen carefully to instruction with a smile or a thoughtful nod. They express gratitude for the help, then they go off and do whatever they want to do. This kind of passive rebellion is more difficult to deal with because it usually goes undiscovered until a crisis occurs. When all hell breaks loose in the person's life we then find that all our careful instruction has gone blissfully unheeded. Some of these folks actually have the ability to convince themselves that hearing advice is the same as doing advice. This is a formula for disaster. James makes this very clear in **JAMES 1:22**.

Some folks have difficulty with the idea of appealing to God for their help. They claim to be willing to do anything except "get religious." They have a reflexive prejudice to spiritual ideas. Sometimes, these are conditioned by bad experiences with churches and church folks. Christians are not always the best representatives of Christ. For many, childhood church was not always a positive experience. Repressive, legalistic ministers have often left a poor picture of God. He is viewed as a grim judge waiting to bring vengeance on the slightest offense. If this is the case, then we are all in serious trouble. The Bible clearly says that we all are deserving of the wrath of God. The point is that He chooses not to pour out wrath, but instead to send His Son to experience our punishment. The whole plan of redemption is designed to hold back judgment.

Others have allowed themselves to become bitter toward God because they believe He has somehow harmed them or let them down. This seems to be most prevalent in those who have lost a loved one, especially a parent. The thinking usually runs something like, "How could a loving God be so unfair as to deprive me of my parent? There are others who deserved to die. Why did he do it to me?" This represents another misunderstanding of things spiritual based on a misbelief about the nature of God. God is not in the business of "taking" people. He is in the business of saving people. We live in a world cursed by the sin of the original man and warped by the continuing disobedience of mankind. Because God sees man as a free moral agent, He does not intervene in the affairs of man unless He is invited through faith-filled prayer according to His Word.

Willingness must include the open-mindedness necessary to rethink ideas about God and about life. It requires an honest appraisal of spiritual

JAMES 1:22
But be doers of the word, and not hearers only, deceiving yourselves.
(New King James)

Don't fool yourself into thinking that you are a listener when you are anything but letting the Word go in one ear and out the other. Act on what you hear.
(Message Bible)

Are you now willing to rethink your ideas about God and life?

reality and a determination to change old attitudes and reactions. This is often the most difficult thing. It may mean overthrowing a lifetime of assumptions about who we are and what we are about. It will mean putting aside prejudices and embracing truth even when truth is unpleasant. Try to remember that your absolute best thinking got you to the condition you are in. It is possible that there are others with a better idea.

1. There are any number of people and agencies ready to give you a hand. Take a look in your yellow pages under "Alcoholism" or "Treatment Facilities" or any other related topic. List at least three phone numbers you think might be possible sources of help.

_____

_____

_____

_____

2. Think over the landscape of your relationships. Do you know anyone who has recovered from an addiction like yours? If so, write down their names and pick the top two as candidates for people to talk with about staying clean and sober.

_____

_____

_____

_____

If you have come to the place of admitting you are addicted, then you have made great progress. If, in addition, you are convinced that you have no hope of recovery in your own ability, then you have traversed a great bit of emotional real estate. Are you now willing to do what it takes to get well? If so, you won't mind taking a few simple actions.

3. Each of us has certain people in our lives whom we greatly admire and respect. For some this would be a teacher, for others a clergyman. Can you name one person in this category to whom you might be willing to turn for counsel?

_____

4. As an act of your willingness to seek help, it is time to pray. It doesn't matter how anti-religious you may be. God will be thrilled to hear from you, but you must be willing to take my word for it. Just ask Him for help, **right now**, out loud.

5. Now it's time to ask another person for help. Choose one of the people or agencies you listed above and call them right now. It doesn't matter what time it is, just make the effort. If you can't reach anyone, look in the Yellow Pages under "Alcohol Treatment" and dial the Alcoholics Anonymous number. If you prefer, you may call our offices at the number on the title page. Another choice might be a local church whose pastor has a good reputation. Just do something and do it NOW. Make a step of commitment to action by contacting someone for help.

Just do something! Do it NOW!

FAITH IN GOD

While the idea of trusting in God may be a quantum leap for many addicts, it is a necessary aspect of a strong recovery. The alternative to God-reliance is self-reliance. This has proved to be a hazardous course for every alcoholic and addict. The fact is that the only hope of genuine recovery is a miraculous intervention of a supernatural type. Simple reform of the old ways is never sufficient to restore the shattered lives of addicts and their families. It requires an actual change of heart, something only God can do.

DOES GOD REALLY EXIST??

PSALM 14:1
Only fools say in their hearts, "There is no God." They are corrupt and their actions are evil; no one does good."

(New Living Translation)

The first problem that confronts many of us as we face the necessity for divine help is the question of God's very existence. We have often avoided this question entirely or have actively opposed the idea. The truth is, however, that every human who is honest with himself knows, or at least wants to believe, that there is something out there which is bigger than he is. The heart of man was created with a desire to know God. Until he does there is unrest in his innermost being.

If you are one who has difficulty with the idea of the existence of a God, but you have made the commitment to willingness, then take the following steps:

1. Make a list of people you know who have a faith in God.

_____

_____

_____

_____

The alternative to God-reliance is self-reliance

2. Pick two names from this list. Go to these individuals and ask them to tell you about their faith and how it developed. Write down anything you find interesting, helpful, or surprising.

_____

_____

_____

_____

_____

_____

_____

3. Get yourself a Bible in a translation which makes sense when you read it. You might consider the New International Version or the New King James Version.

4. Using your new Bible, begin to read and think about at least one scripture reference per day. Begin with the following list. After each scripture reference write out what that verse tells you about the existence of God.

EXAMPLE:

PSALM 10:4 _People who are proud don't seek God. They seem to think and act like there is no God._

PSALM 10:4
The wicked in his proud countenance does not seek God; God is in none of his thoughts.

(New King James)

PSALM 14:1 _____

_____

_____

ROMANS 1:28 _____

ROMANS 1:28
And since they were not open to having God in their thinking, God turned them loose with a closed mind to act like asses.

(Cotton Patch Translation)

_____

_____

_____

ROMANS 1:19-20 _____

_____

_____

_____

PSALM 19:1-6 _____

_____

_____

_____

ISAIAH 40:26 _____

_____

_____

_____

ACTS 14:15-17 _____

_____

_____

_____

ISAIAH 57:15 _____

_____

_____

_____

PSALM 9:9-10
The Lord is a shelter for the oppressed, a refuge in times of trouble. Those who know your name trust in you, for you, O Lord, do not abandon those who search for you.

(New Living Translation)

God's a safe-house for the battered, a sanctuary during bad times. The moment you arrive, you relax; you're never sorry you knocked.

(Message Bible)

Faith in God is a shift in lifestyle reflecting a trust in God. The concept includes a commitment to the will of God, a relationship with the Person of God, a dependence on the grace of God, and an obedience to the command of God.

JOHN 14:6
Jesus said to them, "I am the way, the truth, and the life. No one comes to the Father except through me."

(New King James)

PSALM 9:10 _____
_____
_____
_____

MATTHEW 7:7-12 _____
_____
_____

JEREMIAH 29:11-14 _____
_____
_____
_____

By the time you have finished these exercises you should come to the conclusion that God reveals Himself to those that seek Him. In living out your commitment to willingness, it is time to seek the Lord. This simply means making yourself available to believe. With all the sincerity you can muster, <u>it is time to pray out loud and ask God to reveal Himself to you.</u>

Faith in God is something which goes beyond simply acknowledging His existence. When I say I have faith in my wife, I don't mean that I believe she exists. I mean I know I can depend on her. This faith has arisen over a period of time as I have come to know her intimately, living with her and talking to her on a daily basis, watching how she lives her life. I have trusted her and she has proven trustworthy. When we use the term "faith in God," we mean this kind of living faith. (See definition in box to the right.)

How do we develop this kind of faith? There are many aspects to that answer that will consume the life of the believer, but the path is begun by getting a clear picture of who God is, getting to know His nature, and grasping the direction of His will.

GETTING ACQUAINTED WITH GOD

Many find it difficult to trust God because they don't know who He is. They see Him through the glasses of an old Sunday School teacher or a TV preacher. It is terribly important to get an accurate idea of who He is. God knew this, so He sent us a Book with stories, poems, and songs about Himself. We can refer to the Book to get the story straight from the Source. Do the following exercises to begin an acquaintance with God.

1. Read **JOHN 14:6**. Jesus tells us that He is the only way to the Father. This is a troublesome idea for many, but it is the truth. Man was cut off from God by sin. Jesus came to open the way back. He did this by giving His life as a sacrifice, enduring the judgment which should have been ours. Read each of the following scriptures, then write out what you learn from each one.

1 PETER 3:18 _____ _____

_____

_____

_____

1 JOHN 2:23 _____

_____

_____

_____

HEBREWS 7:25 _____

_____

_____

_____

MATTHEW 11:27-30 _____

_____

_____

_____

1 CORINTHIANS 15:1-7 _____

_____

_____

_____

ROMANS 10:9-10 _____

_____

_____

_____

HEBREWS 7:25
That's why He is forever able to save those who approach God through Him – He's always on the alert to assist them in every way possible.

(Cotton Patch Translation)

ROMANS 10:9-10
If you confess with your mouth that Jesus is Lord and believe in your heart that God raised him from the dead, you will be saved. For it is by believing in your heart that you are made right with God, and it is by confessing with your mouth that you are saved.

(New Living Translation)

My Commitment: I will read the Gospel written by

_____.

When you finish reading the Gospel you have chosen, write the date here:

_____.

2. By this time you have seen that the Bible is clear on the necessity of faith in Christ for relationship with God. Jesus came as God in the flesh. He lived a sinless life in the earth, then was crucified as the substitute for us. He was raised again the third day and ascended into heaven where He now intervenes on our behalf. His request of us is simple: declare Him to be Lord (Master or Ruler) of our individual lives. This is the door of salvation, into relationship with God.

Have you taken this step? This would be a good time to ask Jesus to enter your life, forgive your sin, and be your Lord.

3. The process of getting to know our God is simplified by the realization that Jesus Christ is God in human form. Read **JOHN 14:7-9**. If we want to know God, we can look at Jesus. The life of Jesus on the earth is described in the four Gospels: Matthew, Mark, Luke and John. Pick one of

these books and read a little bit each day to begin to see the nature of God by observing Jesus here on the earth. Put away your preconceived ideas and let the life of Jesus reveal the nature of God.

4. One of the most important ways we get to know anyone is through spending time with them. We have opportunity to do both these things with God. We can spend time with Him by talking to Him in prayer. It is OK to simply speak to Him as you would to a friend for whom you have great respect. He will listen. It is time to begin praying daily. Set aside at least 15 minutes in the morning to talk to God and then be quiet in His presence. Let Him give peace to your heart and guide your thoughts.

5. Another important method for getting acquainted with someone is by listening to what they have to say. In the Bible, we have the words of God recorded in a language we can understand. It is time to look in the Word of God to see what God says about Himself. Read one of these scriptures each day and write out what it tells you about God.

HEBREWS 11:6 _____

_____

_____

_____

PSALM 86:5 _____

_____

_____

_____

DEUTERONOMY 10:17-18 _____

_____

_____

_____

PSALM 99:9 _____

_____

_____

_____

JOHN 4:24 _____

_____

_____

_____

1 CORINTHIANS 1:9
God, who got you started in this spiritual adventure, shares with us the life of His Son and our Master Jesus. He will never give up on you. Never forget that.

(Message Bible)

1 CORINTHIANS 1:9 _____

_____

_____

1 CORINTHIANS 14:33 _____

_____

_____

_____

1 JOHN 1:5 _____

_____

_____

_____

1 JOHN 4:16 _____

_____

_____

_____

TRUSTING GOD

As we get to know God and His nature, we begin to find it easier to trust Him. Faith in God means that we trust Him with our lives. In the beginning, we may be able to trust Him only for our sobriety. As we continue to walk with Him, we will find ourselves able to trust Him in more and more areas of life. Trust in God is the antidote for worry and anxiety. When I am mentally troubled it indicates that I have not placed the concerns of my life in the hands of God. Learning to trust is a process. It takes practice and repeated prayer, but it is a key to peaceful sobriety. It is time to begin forming the habit of trusting in God.

Learning to trust is a process.

1. Look up the following verses. Write out what the Bible tells us to do with our worries.

PHILIPPIANS 4:6-8 _____

_____

_____

_____

_____

MATTHEW 6:25-34 _____

_____

_____

_____

_____

_____

_____

MATTHEW 6:34
Give your entire attention to what God is doing right now, and don't get worked up about what may or may not happen tomorrow. God will help you deal with whatever hard things come up when the time comes.

(Message Bible)

1 PETER 5:6-7 _____

_____
_____
_____
_____
_____
_____
_____

PSALM 37:8 (b)
Do not fret (worry) - it only causes harm.

(New King James)

2. When you find yourself worrying, what is the number one issue you worry about?

_____
_____
_____

In light of the verses about worrying, it is time to pray. Talk to God now about the issues you worry over. Give them to Him, then ask Him for grace to trust. A prayer might sound something like this:

> *Dear Heavenly Father, Please forgive me for worrying about my financial situation. I want to trust You with my finances, so I ask You for grace to trust them to You. Thank You.*
> *Amen.*

OBEYING GOD

Another part of faith in God has to do with obeying the will of God in our lives. In the beginning of our life with Him, finding His will may seem a mystery. It really isn't, but we don't see as clearly today as we will tomorrow. Today we begin by obeying the part we know and trusting Him for the part He will reveal later. We know it is the will of God that we stay clean and sober, so we can start there. In addition to this, Jesus provided us with one simple commandment, to love one another as He loved us. We can make a good start on this path of obedience by simply staying straight and attempting to love others.

PRAY

1. As surely as you have made a determination to remain drug and alcohol free, you will be tempted to fall back. You have several tools to help you when this happens. The first is simply asking God for help in staying clean and sober. Start your day with that prayer. If you haven't done that, you might want to do it now.

2. The second tool in your tool kit is the ability to say "NO." Read

JAMES 4:7. You have made a commitment to God, now when temptation comes you can resist it and expect it to go away. How do you resist? Take a look at the example Jesus gave us in **MATTHEW 4:1-11**. When He was tempted, He spoke directly to the devil and told him what the Bible said. When you are tempted, you can do the same. With each scripture listed write out what you would say to resist the temptation to drink or use drugs.

JAMES 4:7 _____

_____

_____

_____

COLOSSIANS 1:13-14 _____

_____

_____

_____

PHILIPPIANS 2:9-11_____

_____

_____

_____

JAMES 4:7
So let God work His will in you. Yell a loud no to the devil and watch him scamper.

(Message Bible)

3. A third very effective tool is found in **JAMES 5:16**. When temptation comes, call someone who knows what you are going through and who also knows how to pray. Let them encourage you and pray with you. You have the support of other believers to help you stay free. Use it. It is important to develop relationships with people who are serious about sobriety and about God. *Choose your associates well.*

 Read: • **PROVERBS 9:6**
  • **PROVERBS 13:20**
  • **1 CORINTHIANS 15:33**

JAMES 5:16
Make this your common practice: confess your sins to each other and pray for each other so that you can live together whole and healed. The prayer of a person living right with God is something powerful to be reckoned with.

(Message Bible)

Make a list of three acquaintances who would be able to help you in time of temptation. List their names and phone numbers.

_____

_____

_____

Now list those associates whom you know to be a bad influence. Stay away from these people unless one of the three on the previous list is with you.

_____

_____

_____

Remember love is not an emotion. It is a commandment.

4. God has given us a clear command that we must love everyone, even our enemies. This is a very tall order. It will require His help. Help given by God to assist us in fulfilling His commands is called "grace." You will need much grace to love some people. Remember love is not an emotion. It is a commandment. Therefore we can love even when we don't feel like it. We can act lovingly even when we feel bitterness. This is not hypocrisy when it is done as an act of obedience to God.

Read **MATTHEW 5:43-48**. Jesus gives us a list of things to do in order to love those who are our enemies. Make a list of people you feel great bitterness, even hatred, toward.

Take each of these names and ask God to bless them with all the best of His kingdom. Pray for their health and wealth and the blessing of their families. Continue to do this daily. This is good spiritual exercise.

Sobriety is not a destination, it is a journey.

If you have been even modestly diligent in these exercises, you have made a good beginning in the life of faith. There is yet much to learn, but you started forming some good habits. Remember the principles you have learned and begin applying them in daily life. Sobriety is not a destination, it is a journey. You have begun a new road which will be exciting and challenging if you will stay the course.

ACCOUNTABILITY

To be accountable means to be obliged to account for one's actions, to bear responsibility for decisions and behaviors. All of us will one day be accountable to God, but that kind of accountability in a distant future is usually insufficient to sway the behavior of a drunkard or an addict. We need the help of other human beings to maintain our sobriety. We need regular relationship with people with whom we are honest and for whom we have respect. It is important that we care what they think.

We need the help of other human beings to maintain our sobriety.

Developing accountable relationships is difficult in our present day. We have all been programmed that it is desirable to "do our own thing." Unfortunately, your "thing" is terribly destructive. You have done it so long and so often that you are no longer doing it, it is doing you. You have lost the power of choice and will need help in the process of restoring that power. In the beginning of sobriety it is entirely possible that the uncomfortable prospect of telling another person that you have fallen off the wagon is the only thing that will keep you on it.

One very popular place of accountability is the support group. This may be Alcoholics Anonymous, or any one of the other support groups available today. There is nothing wrong with going to these groups. It is important to remember that the purpose of secular support groups is to maintain sobriety, not to develop in our Christian life. See *"God Help Me, I Can't Stop!"* for more information on Alcoholics Anonymous for the Christian.

DEVELOPING ACCOUNTABLE RELATIONSHIPS

Remember: the purpose of secular support groups is to maintain sobriety, not to develop our Christian life.

There are many Christian-oriented support groups available today. A number of local churches have their own versions. There are also national organizations such as Alcoholics Victorious and Overcomers Anonymous which can offer much assistance. As a step of willingness, it is time to investigate some of your options for developing accountable relationships in support groups.

1. Call your local Alcoholics Anonymous or Narcotics Anonymous number and find out about meetings near you. List three which you could possibly attend. Be sure to list times and locations.

_____

_____

_____

2. Call three area churches or para-church organizations and ask if they know of any Christian-oriented recovery groups or programs in your area. List the three and their responses.

_____

_____

_____

_____

_____

_____

THE DREADED "S" WORD: SUBMISSION

In discussing Christian relationships, the Bible frequently uses the word "submission." The word means to offer oneself as a subordinate or to obey. This is a distasteful concept to most addicts. We generally don't like the idea of being instructed or subservient. We are proud people. In order to become eligible for many of the promises of God, we must first humble ourselves.

Read each of the following passages and note what it says to you.

1. PROVERBS 16:18-19 _____

_____

_____

1 PETER 5:7
Let Him in on all your problems, because you mean much to Him.

(Cotton Patch Translation)

2. MATTHEW 18:3 _____

_____

_____

1 PETER 5:5-7
And you who are younger must follow your leaders. But all of you, leaders and followers alike, are to be down to earth with each other, for – God has had it with the proud, but takes delight in just plain people. So be content with who you are and don't put on airs. God's strong hand is on you; He'll promote you at the right time. Live carefree before God; He is most careful with you.

(Message Bible)

3. Notice in **1 PETER 5:5** the relationship between submission and humility.

> *Likewise you younger people submit yourselves to your elders. Yes, all of you be submissive to one another, and be clothed with humility, for God resists the proud, but gives grace to the humble.*

(New King James)

In this case Peter is talking about submitting to those who are our elders in the Lord. This is a powerful concept. It is a wise Christian who seeks to establish relationships with those who are older and wiser in the things of God. There are many scriptures which refer to submitting to people in the Body of Christ as a token of our submission to the Lord. Read each of the following passages and write what it says to you.

1 PETER 5:5-6 _____

JAMES 4:7 _____

EPHESIANS 5:21 _____

HEBREWS 13:17
*Be responsive to your
pastoral leaders. Listen
to their counsel. They are
alert to the condition of
your lives and work under
the strict supervision of
God. Contribute to the
joy of their leadership,
not its drudgery. Why
would you want to make
things hard for them?*
(Message Bible)

HEBREWS 13:17 _____

1 CORINTHIANS 16:16 _____

FINDING A CHURCH

As Christians, we are encouraged to develop submitted relationships with other members of the Body of Christ. This does not necessarily mean we will do everything they say, but it does mean we will discuss our decisions with them and consider their opinion as very important. The group of people to whom we should submit includes our spouse, other believers, and those in leadership in our churches. In order for you to do this, you must first find a church, then take a submitted attitude toward your pastor and those to whom he delegates authority. You need to have open, honest relationship with some trusted elder believers. In order to achieve this, here are some exercises to undertake.

1. From the three churches you previously called, visit the organizations they recommended. Write out your impressions of each group and give the name of the person who impressed you the most.

1. _____

2. _____

_____

_____

_____

3. _____

_____

_____

_____

    2. Begin searching for a church to attend regularly. You should look for one which has some specific ministry to those with addictions. Inquire with the church office, then visit their service. You will want a church where the Bible is used to read and preach, and where they believe in salvation through faith in the work of Jesus Christ as a sacrifice for the sins of the world. What are the characteristics you look for in finding a church?

1 . **2 TIMOTHY 2:4** **EPHESIANS 4:11-12**	Preaching of the Word and preparation of the people for ministry.
2 . **HEBREWS 10:24-25**	Corporate meetings which encourage love and good works.
3 . **1 CORINTHIANS 12:25-26**	Empathy and concrete help for those in need or trouble.
4 . **1 CORINTHIANS 12:3-11**	The presence of the Holy Spirit in all His manifestations.

Are there other characteristics which are important to you? List them.

_____

_____

_____

_____

_____

_____

    3. When you find a church where you think you might be comfortable and which has some program for addictions, call the pastor and make an appointment for counseling. Tell him exactly what you are doing. Tell him you are an addict or an alcoholic and you are looking for someone to whom you can be accountable. If he has good concrete advice, is willing to refer you to someone for ongoing counsel, or is willing to continue to see you himself, you can begin to get involved in the church.

    4. Look for opportunities to serve where you will work side by side with others. Try cleaning the building, mowing the lawn, attending men's or ladies' fellowships, or anything else where good relationships may be

HEBREWS 10:24-25
Think of ways to encourage one another to outbursts of love and good deeds. And let us not neglect our meeting together as some people do, but encourage and warn each other, especially now that the day of His coming back again is drawing near.
(New Living Translation)

And let's think up ways to provoke everybody into "fits of love and kindness"...
(Cotton Patch Translation)

Write down the pastor's name and the time when you will meet with him or his designee.

_____

_____

_____

_____

_____

established. Ask the pastor or your counselor for other ideas. Write here what you plan to do and when you plan to do it.

_____

_____

_____

_____

5. It is important to choose friends carefully before you develop accountable relationships. Look up each scripture and write out what it means in the choice of a friend.

PROVERBS 13:20 _____

_____

_____

_____

PROVERBS 28:7
Young people who obey the law are wise; those who seek out worthless companions bring shame to their parents.

(New Living Translation)

PROVERBS 28:7 _____

_____

_____

_____

_____

PROVERBS 4:14-19 _____

_____

_____

_____

PROVERBS 9:6 _____

_____

_____

_____

1 CORINTHIANS 15:32-33
…"Let's feast and get drunk, for tomorrow we die." Don't be fooled by those who say such things, for "bad company corrupts good character."

(New Living Translation)

1 CORINTHIANS 15:33 _____

_____

_____

_____

PROVERBS 23:19-21 _____

_____

_____

_____

SUBMIT YOURSELVES TO ONE ANOTHER
(EPHESIANS 5:21)

Choose your friends carefully. They may mark the difference between life and death someday. **JAMES 5:16** encourages us to confess our faults to one another and pray for one another that we may be healed. When you have found other believers who are serious about the things of God, you will want to tell them of your addiction. You need not tell all the details of your behavior, but as much as you are comfortable in disclosing. Establish as many prayer resources as you can.

EPHESIANS 5:21
submitting to one another in the fear of God.
(New Living Translation)

Put yourselves under one another with Christ-like respect.
(Cotton Patch Translation)

1. List the names and phone numbers of all the people you know to whom you feel you can turn to talk seriously when you are troubled or tempted.

_____

_____

_____

_____

2. From your list, pick two and call them to find time to meet with them for coffee. It is time to get serious about accountability. Note your appointments here.

_____

_____

_____

3. Attend services at the church you have chosen. Attend Sunday and at least one other service during the week. Do this for one month. For every service you attend, write down the one most important point you got out of the service.

SERVICE #1 _____

_____

_____

SERVICE #2 _____

_____

_____

SERVICE #3 _____

_____

_____

_____

SERVICE #4 _____

_____

_____

_____

SERVICE #5 _____

_____

_____

_____

SERVICE #6 _____

_____

_____

_____

SERVICE #7 _____

_____

_____

_____

SERVICE #8 _____

_____

_____

_____

SELF-EXAMINATION

Self-examination is the process of taking a dispassionate look at our own actions and motives. The purpose is to change our thinking and learn to live free from self-centeredness. This is contrary to human nature. It is a discipline which must be taught, learned, and practiced until it becomes a habit. This principle lies at the heart of happy sobriety and is the linchpin of spiritual and emotional growth.

2 CORINTHIANS 13:5
Examine yourselves to see if your faith is really genuine.

(New Living Translation)

"EXAMINE YOURSELVES..."

1. The natural tendency of every human being is to attempt to blame others for their failures and shortcomings. In the case of the addict, this is especially pronounced. He is an expert on self-deception, projection, denial, and blame. To overcome this requires the willingness to be rigorously honest before God and before other human beings. Look up each of the following scriptures. In each passage notice who is being blamed.

GENESIS 3:12
Yes, Adam admitted, but it was the woman you gave me who brought me to the fruit and I ate.

(New Living Translation)

GENESIS 3:12. Have you ever blamed your spouse for your actions? If so, describe the incident and tell the truth about who was at fault.

_____
_____
_____
_____
_____

GENESIS 3:13
Then the Lord God asked the woman, "How could you do such a thing?" "The serpent tricked me," she replied. "That's why I ate it."

(New Living Translation)

GENESIS 3:13. Who does Eve blame for her sin? _____

Do you think this is a reasonable accusation? Why or why not?

_____
_____
_____
_____
_____

Read **EXODUS 32**. This chapter recounts the famous story of the golden calf. Notice verses **21-25**. Who does Aaron blame for this incident?

_____
_____
_____
_____

Read **1 SAMUEL 15**. Here we have the account of Saul's failure to destroy all the spoil of the Amalekites as he had been instructed by God. Notice verses **15** and **21**. Who does Saul blame? _____

_____

_____

In both these last two instances, we see very powerful men blaming pressure from others for their own wrongdoing. Can you think of instances when you have done things which you knew to be wrong because you wanted to appease or please other people? (We sometimes refer to this as peer pressure.) Describe three such instances.

1. _____

_____

_____

_____

2. _____

_____

_____

_____

3. _____

_____

_____

_____

2. Go back and read **GENESIS 3:12** again. Notice the implication of Adam. He blamed "The woman who You gave." Though he directly blames Eve, his real accusation is toward God. If only God had not given him this defective woman he would not have had to commit this offense. This is a prime ploy of most addicts. In the end it is all really God's fault. He gave us the wrong parents. He let us be born in the wrong skin. He didn't give us enough money. He took a parent from our home. He allowed us to be ill. He generally hasn't run our lives as He should. This is a poor excuse. Job was guilty of this practice, but he was corrected in no uncertain terms. Read **JOB 34:5-15.**

GENESIS 3:12
Yes, Adam admitted, but it was the woman you gave me who brought me the fruit and I ate.

(New Living Translation)

3. The difficulties in our lives are never to be blamed on God. This is a poor religious cop-out to avoid dealing with our own circumstances. The world we live in is already cursed when we arrive in it. Because of Adam's sin, the whole world is under the power of Satan. There is a curse on the earth which causes all kinds of problems. Every person who lives in this world has to deal with the effects of Adam's sin in his own particular circumstance. Read each of the following scriptures and write out what each tells you about the state of the world in which we live.

2 CORINTHIANS 4:4
Satan, the god of this evil world, has blinded the minds of those who don't believe, so they are unable to see the glorious light of the Good News that is shining upon them. They don't understand the message we preach about the glory of Christ, who is the exact likeness of God.

(New Living Translation)

2 CORINTHIANS 4:4 _____

_____

_____

_____

_____

1 JOHN 5:19 _____

_____

_____

_____

JOHN 3:18 _____

_____

_____

_____

_____

4. Adam's sin is not the only cause of trouble in this life. In addition to the difficulties which are ours because we live in this world, we all have difficulties which are ours because we have sown seed. Much of what happens in our life today is the result of the seed we sowed yesterday. Seed can come in many forms: attitudes, words, money, or deeds. No matter what the seed, there is always a harvest in life. Notice the following verses. For each one, discuss how the principle in the passage might apply to your life.

GALATIANS 6:7
Don't be mislead. Remember that you can't ignore God and get away with it. You will always reap what you sow.

(New Living Translation)

Don't let anyone pull the wool over your eyes – you can't turn up your nose at God! For a man harvests exactly what he plants.

(Cotton Patch Translation)

GALATIANS 6:7 _____

_____

_____

_____

_____

PROVERBS 1:24-32 _____

_____

_____

_____

_____

_____

You reap what you sow
or
what goes around comes around!

PROVERBS 6:14-15 _____

_____

_____

_____

PROVERBS 11:18 _____

_____

_____

LUKE 6:35-38 _____

_____

_____

2 CORINTHIANS 9:6-8 _____

_____

_____

5. The essence of following Christ is taking responsibility for our own actions. Until we are willing to admit our wrongs we are condemned to suffer their consequences. The moment we are ready to admit our wrongdoing, the blood of Jesus washes us clean. (Notice **1 JOHN 1:9**) Our assignment as Christians is always to avoid judging others while we examine ourselves, paying attention to both action and motive.

Notice **MATTHEW 7:1-5**. We all like to pull out the admonition, "judge not" when someone disapproves of our behavior. Most of us have used phrases like "Who are you to judge me?" It is a great way to deflect attention from ourselves and put people on the defensive. The intent of the passage, however, is not to condone sinful behavior and exempt everyone from being corrected. The Lord is telling us that before we correct someone else, we must be sure our own eye is clear. An eye fogged by judgment prevents us from carefully removing the injurious material from our brother's eye. Love never leaves the splinter in the eye of its brother. It always removes it with tender, loving care. The idea is to judge self first, then help others. Notice also the following scriptures. Give your own idea of how they apply to you.

1 CORINTHIANS 11:31 _____

_____

_____

2 CORINTHIANS 13:5 _____

_____

_____

_____

1 JOHN 1:9
…if we admit our sins – make a clean breast of them – He won't let us down. He'll be true to Himself. He'll forgive our sins and purge us of all wrongdoing.

(Message Bible)

But if we confess our sins to Him, He is faithful and just to forgive us and to cleanse us from every wrong.

(New Living Translation)

MATTHEW 7:1-5
"Don't pick on people, jump on their failures, criticize their faults unless, of course, you want the same treatment. That critical spirit has a way of boomeranging. It's easy to see a smudge on your neighbor's face and be oblivious to the ugly sneer on your own. Do you have the nerve to say, 'Let me wash your face for you,' when your own face is distorted by contempt? It's this whole traveling road-show mentality all over again, playing a holier-than-thou part instead of just living your part. Wipe that ugly sneer off your own face, and you might be fit to offer a washcloth to your neighbor.

(Message Bible)

6. In the process of judging ourselves, we must avoid becoming bogged down in guilt for past sins. As believers in Jesus Christ, our old sins have been cleansed. We are not looking at them in order to beat ourselves for our evil behavior. Old things have passed away, behold all things have become new. What we are looking for is old patterns of behavior, faulty attitudes, and ungodly thinking which are affecting our lives in the present.

Read the following passages. Write out what each tells you about what happened to you when you were born again.

JOHN 3:3-7 _____

_____

_____

_____

2 CORINTHIANS 5:17
Therefore if anyone is in Christ, he is a new creation; old things have passed away; behold, all things have become new.

(New King James)

2 CORINTHIANS 5:17 _____

_____

_____

_____

PSALM 51:9-12 _____

_____

_____

_____

EZEKIEL 36:26-27 _____

_____

_____

_____

ISAIAH 43:25
I – yes, I alone – am the one who blots our your sins for my own sake and will never think of them again.

(New Living Translation)

ISAIAH 43:25 _____

_____

_____

_____

7. Although we are washed clean by the blood of Jesus Christ, and we have become new creatures in Him, we still have remnants of our old life to deal with. The Bible tells us that we will need to deal especially with the way we think. Our thinking, including our attitudes and prejudices, will control our emotions. Our emotions often run our lives. The process of changing the way we think is part of our commission for the rest of our lives.

Look up the following passages and write out what they say about your thinking. What is the Lord asking us to do?

ISAIAH 55:7-8 _____

_____

_____

_____

2 CORINTHIANS 10:5 _____

_____

_____

_____

ROMANS 12:2 _____

_____

_____

_____

8. We face the problem of identifying the thoughts we have which are in need of change. How do I know I am suffering from wrong thinking? Certainly, we see areas that need change as we look into the Word of God. If we are honest, there are many places where our old thinking is contrary to God's Word. When we see these areas we must ask God to help us change.

Painful and distressing emotions can also be a tool in identifying faulty thinking. Like red lights on the dashboard of a car, our emotional responses often indicate there is trouble under the hood. There is a simple rule of thumb which we can apply: _"If I am disturbed, there is something wrong with me."_ When the emotional red lights of resentment, fear, self-pity, or despair begin to flash, we need to look under our hood and examine our thinking. The rule is always to examine myself and not others.

We want to look at these four offenders: fear, resentment, self-pity, and discouragement. What do these emotions tell us about ourselves? What can we do to correct our faulty thinking?

FEAR

God never leads the believer with fear. He is a God of peace. When we experience fear, we are simply seeing evidence of an area where our trust in God is weak. Fear is almost always a self-centered emotion. Our internal concerns sound something like "What will happen to **me**?" or "Am **I** going to lose something?" or "Will **I** not receive what **I** think should be **mine**?" Our self-esteem, our finances, our security, or our personal relations are threatened and we are afraid.

God is unalterably opposed to our being afraid. He wants to be the sole controller of our lives. He wants our obedience to spring out of a heart of love and gratitude to Him. When we suffer fear of other things, we often act based on our fears. These are areas where God cannot control our lives. He has said many things in His Word which make His attitude clear.

1. Here is a list of scriptures dealing with the subject of fear. Look them up and use them as your daily devotion material for the next few days. Write down what you learned from the scripture.

ROMANS 12:2
Don't copy the behavior and customs of this world, but let God transform you into a new person by changing the way you think. Then you will know what God wants you to do and you will know how good and pleasing and perfect His will really is.

(New Living Translation)

There is a simple rule of thumb which we can apply: "If I am disturbed, there is something wrong with me."

PSALM 23:4
Even when I walk through the dark valley of death, I will not be afraid, for you are close beside me. Your rod and Your staff protect and comfort me.

(New Living Translation)

PSALM 23:4 _____
_____
_____
_____

MATTHEW 10:29-31 _____
_____
_____
_____

HEBREWS 13:5-6 _____
_____
_____
_____

ROMANS 8:15 _____
_____
_____
_____

ISAIAH 41:10 _____
_____
_____
_____

1 JOHN 4:18 _____
_____
_____
_____

LUKE 12:32 _____
_____
_____
_____

PSALM 118:6
God's now at my side and I'm not afraid; who would dare lay a hand on me?

(Message Bible)

PSALM 118:6 _____
_____
_____
_____

HEBREWS 2:15 _____
_____
_____
_____

PROVERBS 29:25 _____
_____
_____
_____

PSALM 27:1-3 _____

_____

_____

LUKE 12:7 _____

_____

_____

_____

PROVERBS 3:25 _____

_____

_____

_____

2 TIMOTHY 1:7 _____

_____

_____

_____

2. Having read and seriously considered all the above information, write a summary of what you have learned about fear, God, and you.

_____

_____

_____

_____

_____

_____

_____

_____

2 TIMOTHY 1:7
For God has not given us a spirit of fear and timidity, but of power, love, and self-discipline.
(New Living Translation)

For God has not given us the heart of a coward but of a strong man filled with love and self-discipline.
(Cotton Patch Translation)

3. It is often easier for us to deal with things if we have some sort of structure to use. Try using the following table, as an example, to list and analyze your fears. In the first column, identify what you are afraid of–the event or the person which inspires the fear. In the second column write in what it is in you that is threatened. Are you fearful about finances? Is your self-esteem threatened? Are your personal relationships (including sex) in danger? In column three, go to the Bible and find what God says about your specific fear. If it's your self-worth, you might look for scriptures which establish God's estimate of your value. If it's personal finances, you can find promises of provision. Be thorough in listing all the recurring fears you can think of.

Examine Yourself

I am afraid of:	It threatens my:	But God says:
1. *EXAMPLE:* Lay-offs at the plant. I might lose my job.	1. Security, self-esteem	1. Philippians 4:19 - My God supplies my needs. Luke 12:7 - I am of great value to God.
2.		
3.		

SPECIFIC STEPS TO OVERCOME FEAR

A. Use the chart to identify the source of the fear.

B. Ask God to forgive you for your self-centeredness.

C. Find God's promise (His Word) concerning your specific fear.

D. Speak the promise aloud every time you begin to feel the fear.

E. Pray for grace to walk ahead, and face your fear head on. This means doing what you are afraid to do or going where you are afraid to go. You must cease to allow fear to control your life. Your life belongs to God. If necessary get a friend in the Lord to walk with you to face the fear.

Faith comes by hearing the Word of God and is made effective when we act on it. Fear comes by hearing the lie of Satan and becomes effective the same way.

RESENTMENT

"Resentment" comes from the Latin meaning "to feel again."

Any ill-will on my part which goes beyond the immediate circumstance is a sign that I am harboring resentment. I need to forgive and forget. Any event which continues to evoke anger after the passage of time is an area where forgiveness is needed. The word "resentment" comes from the Latin meaning "to feel again." A resentment is an area of anger which keeps coming back. When the re-telling of an incident evokes intense feeling after the passage of time, I may need to forgive. Sometimes we are easily angered by people, events, or words which remind us of past pain or bitterness. We may overreact to today's events because we are still smarting from yesterday. This is resentment. A short temper today is often the result of a fuse already ignited by yesterday's anger.

1. Once again, the Bible gives us God's opinion on our resentment. He is in favor of our forgiving all those who harm us no matter the offense.

This is because our unforgiveness shuts us off from the full blessing of the Spirit. It grieves the very Holy Spirit who dwells in us. It hinders our prayer life and causes damage to those around us.

Look up the following passages and write what they imply about the problems caused by unforgiveness:

EPHESIANS 4:30-32 _____

_____

_____

_____

MARK 11:22-26 _____

_____

_____

_____

HEBREWS 12:15 _____

_____

_____

_____

HEBREWS 12:15
Keep a sharp eye out for weeds of bitter discontent. A thistle or two gone to seed can ruin a whole garden in no time.

(Message Bible)

2. Read the story in **MATTHEW 18:21-35**. Notice the grounds on which we are asked to forgive. The call is to forgive based on the fact that we have been forgiven a great debt. The only payment we are asked is that we forgive those who trespass against us. When we understand the forgiveness that is ours in Jesus Christ, we can begin to find the grace to forgive those who have offended us. Notice also the penalty for unforgiveness: TORMENT. The most miserable people in the world are those who never learn to release their debtors and allow God to deal with them.

The drive for vengeance is a poisonous snake in the human heart whose venom poisons its host and all those around him.

STEPS TO OVERCOME RESENTMENT

The penalty for unforgiveness: TORMENT

A. Using the same type of chart we used for identifying fears, make a list of all those toward whom you feel malice. Include the offense which caused the anger. Again, look at your own heart to see what in you has been offended—self-esteem (pride), security, relationships, etc. You will find that many of your resentments go back to a core of fear. The works of darkness in the human soul seem varied, but they all spring from the same evil root of self-centeredness.

B. In looking at the offense, take a moment to admit if there is any fault of your own in the matter. If there is, ask the Lord's forgiveness for your own wrongdoing.

EPHESIANS 4:31, 32
Let every scrap of bitterness and resentment and anger and loud talk and running down of others be put away from you, along with all other evil. Deal gently with one another and maintain a good attitude. Show goodwill toward each other as God showed toward you in Christ.

(Cotton Patch Translation)

1 CORINTHIANS 10:13
But remember that the temptations that come into your life are not different from what others experience. And God is faithful. He will keep the temptation from becoming so strong that you can't stand up against it. When you are tempted, He will show you a way out so that you will not give in to it.
(Message Bible)

No test or temptation that comes your way is beyond the course of what others have had to face. All you need to remember is that God will never let you down; He'll never let you be pushed past your limit; He'll always be there to help you come through it.
(New Living Translation)

C. For each person on the list (and this may be a long list), make a conscious decision to forgive them as an act of obedience to the Lord. Remember, forgiveness is not an emotion, it is a commandment. It must come from a decision. The feelings will follow. Notice **EPHESIANS 4:31-32** and **1 JOHN 4:7-11**.

D. Read **MATTHEW 5:43-45**. Begin praying for your offenders. Ask the Lord to bless them with every spiritual and earthly blessing. This is an act of faith and does not require that you feel as if you are sincere. You are sincere in your desire to obey God. That is sufficient.

E. Go to **1 JOHN 1:9**. Ask the Lord to forgive you of the bitterness you have harbored. It is sin.

F. Think of ways to be a blessing to those who have harmed you. If, as a result of your bitterness, you have harmed them in some way, you may need to ask their forgiveness.

SELF-PITY

Feeling sorry for ourselves is the basis of most depression. When we begin to moan about our condition and believe that our lot in life is somehow worse than that of others, we are in dangerous territory. It is but a short leap to questioning the justice of God. Blaming God instead of believing God keeps us in our bondage. God is always our solution, not our problem. **1 CORINTHIANS 10:13** tells us that whatever our test and trial, it is common to man. This means we are not alone or unique. When we begin to feel sorry for ourselves we are in the grip of pride of the worst sort.

Self-pity puts us in a spiritual danger zone. The scripture is full of warnings against this disease.

1. Self-pity accuses God of being unjust. Find at least three scriptures which tells us that God is just.

_____

_____

_____

2. Self-pity is always selfish. This is contrary to the command of love. Read **JOHN 15:12-14**. What does it mean to you to "lay down your life for your friends"?

_____

_____

_____

_____

3. Self-pity is full of complaint rather than faith. This destroys our witness and blocks the blessing of God. Read **PHILIPPIANS 2:14-16**.

4. Self-pity saps our motivation to carry on, often stopping us just short of the victory God plans for us. It gives us the idea that we are somehow flawed beyond the ability of God to help us or that He is less gracious to us than He is to others. This was Job's problem. Read **JOB 34:5-15**. It also attacked Elijah. Read **1 KINGS 19:1-4**.

5. Self-pity prevents us from taking responsibility for our own actions and outcomes. The essence of Christianity is to "take up your cross and follow Me." Until we claim the ownership of our own failings and the responsibility for changing our own actions, we will never be able to fulfill the will of God. Until we claim our sins as our own, they can never be removed. Read **LUKE 9:23-24** and **1 JOHN 1:5-10**.

STEPS TO OVERCOME SELF-PITY

A. Using the same basic methods as for fear and resentment, identify areas of self-pity. Finish the sentence, "I feel sorry for myself because......" You might try listening to your complaints for a day to identify problem areas.

B. Find the promises in the Word which apply to your situation and begin to claim the promise rather than complaining the problem. You might pray like this:

> *Father, my marriage is real stormy and I don't like it. ISAIAH 32:18 says that I should live in a peaceable habitation. You promised it and I claim it. Thank You for a peaceful house.*

C. Gratitude is God's perfect antidote for self-pity. We are designed to be creatures of praise, resounding with the goodness of God.

Read: **1 THESSALONIANS 5:18**
   EPHESIANS 5:18-21
   PHILIPPIANS 4:6-7

Make a list of all you have to be grateful for. Be specific: "I can walk, I can breathe, I can write, I have friends, I am saved, ..."

_____
_____
_____
_____
_____
_____
_____

ISAIAH 32:18
My people will live in safety, quietly at home. They will be at rest.
(New Living Translation)

1 THESSALONIANS 5:18
No matter what happens, always be thankful, for this is God's will for you who belong to Christ Jesus.
(New Living Translation)

Thank God no matter what happens. This is the way God wants you who belong to Christ Jesus to live.
(Message Bible)

D. Review your list, and when self-pity starts to rear its ugly head, recount your gratitude list and thank God aloud for what He has given you.

The best way to get free from self is to do something selfless.

E. Read **JOHN 13:1-17**. When Jesus was facing death in the greatest injustice of all time, He didn't think of Himself. He found the opportunity to serve and teach the fickle friends who would soon deny Him in His moment of trial. Self-pity is the opposite of love. Find someone to help and help them. The best way to get free from self is to do something selfless. Record your experience here. How did it make you feel?

F. Self-pity is an ugly thing. It is unbecoming a child of God. When you catch yourself at it, ask God to forgive you and deal with it swiftly and without mercy.

DISCOURAGEMENT

To discourage literally means to remove the courage from the heart.

We have a number of terms which we use to describe the state of discouragement: despair, disheartened, dismayed, hopeless, etc. Webster says it means to be deprived of courage, hope or confidence. To discourage literally means to remove the courage from the heart. One of the ploys of the enemy is to convince the Christian that he lacks the necessary strength, determination, or skill to fulfill the plan of God. He does this through the intimidation of circumstances and the destruction of negative words.

1. The Bible is full of wonderful examples of discouragement and the power of God to overcome it. The Children of Israel became discouraged because of the difficulty of the ways they had to travel. Read **NUMBERS 21:4-9**. Notice the symptoms of discouragement:

- they spoke against God,

- they spoke against their spiritual mentors,

- they looked with longing on the land they had left, and

- they complained about the quality of God's amazing provision.

Do you see any of these symptoms in your life? Make a list of things you are discouraged about, areas where you have given up hope.

_____
_____
_____
_____
_____
_____
_____

2. Another wonderful example of becoming discouraged is Israel at the Jordan when the twelve spies brought a bad report. Read Moses' account of this in **DEUTERONOMY 1:19-33**. God repeatedly told them, "Do not fear or be discouraged." In spite of this, they listened to the report of ten men and became discouraged in their hearts. Go back to **NUMBERS** chapters **13** and **14** to read the full account of this incident. Now notice especially **NUMBERS 13:31-33**. Here we see the ploys Satan uses to cause us to give way to discouragement and despair.

VERSE 31: _"They are stronger than we..."_ They fell into the trap of comparing the problem to their own resources to solve it. We must remember that our problems are to be measured against God's ability, not our own. For each of the areas of discouragement you noted above, find a promise that speaks to the problem.

NUMBERS 13:31
...we can't attack these people, they're way stronger than we are.
(Message Bible)

_____
_____
_____
_____
_____
_____
_____

VERSE 32: _"The land is a land which devours its inhabitants."_ Discouragement is often accompanied and made worse when we "awful-ize" the situation. That means we exaggerate the problem using terms like "worst," "biggest," or "always." When we find ourselves recounting our problem, do we sometimes make it bigger than it really is? Go back over your list and re-state each problem exactly as it is.

NUMBERS 13:32
...They spread scarey rumors among the people of Israel. They said, "We scouted out the land from one end to the other – it's a land that swallows people whole.
(Message Bible)

_____
_____
_____
_____

NUMBERS 13:33
...and they looked down on us as if we were grasshoppers.
(Message Bible)

VERSE 33: *"We were like grasshoppers in our own eyes."* Discouragement usually reflects how we look at ourselves. As you face your problems, how are you seeing yourself? Are you weak, ineffective, and frightened? Or are you victorious, empowered and full of wisdom? What does the scripture say about you? What will you choose to believe?

_____

_____

NUMBERS 13:33
...alongside them we felt like grasshoppers.

(Message Bible)

VERSE 33: *"And so were we in theirs."* The way we see ourselves will determine how we are viewed by the enemy. Satan loves to find believers who report constantly on their own weaknesses. It lets him know that this individual is expecting to fight the battle in their own strength and he can do very much what he likes. When the enemy assaults our mind it is important to let him hear what we believe.

Say this: *I am a child of God empowered by the Holy Spirit and doing business in the Name of Jesus.*

3. Read the following scriptures and record what we can learn about discouragement (the Old Testament often uses the word "dismayed" instead of discouraged).

COLOSSIANS 3:21 _____

_____

_____

DEUTERONOMY 31:7-8 _____

_____

_____

JOSHUA 1:9
Have I not commanded you? Be strong and of good courage; do not be afraid, nor be dismayed, for the LORD your God is with you wherever you go.

(New King James)

JOSHUA 1:9 _____

_____

_____

1 SAMUEL 17:11 _____

_____

_____

1 CHRONICLES 28:20 _____

_____

_____

2 CHRONICLES 20:15-17 _____

_____

_____

_____

STEPS TO OVERCOME DISCOURAGEMENT

A. Using the inventory method, identify the thinking which is causing you to feel hopeless.

B. Identify the circumstances or words which are intimidating you.

C. Find the promise that fits your situation and begin to speak the promise. You can also make a list of victories the Lord has given you in the past and recount them. This can be a very encouraging thing. Read **1 SAMUEL 30:6**.

> **1 SAMUEL 30:6**
> *And suddenly David was in worse trouble. There was talk among the men, bitter over the loss of their families, of stoning him. David strengthened himself with trust in his God.*
>
> (Message Bible)

_____

_____

_____

_____

D. Write a plan for change. Discuss with a trusted friend how to overcome your circumstance. Take a step of action. Immobility is the devil's trap for the discouraged. Read **2 KINGS 7:3-5**.

_____

_____

_____

_____

> **2 KINGS 7:3-5**
> *It happened that four lepers were sitting just outside the city gate. They said to one another, "What are we doing sitting here at death's door? If we enter the famine-struck city we'll die; if we stay here we'll die. So let's take our chances in the camp of Aram and throw ourselves on their mercy. If they receive us we'll live, if they kill us we'll die. We've got nothing to lose." So after the sun went down they got up and went to the camp of Aram. When they got to the edge of the camp, surprise! Not a man in the camp!*
>
> (Message Bible)

THE GREAT PRINCIPLE OF INVENTORY

Remember that inventory, self-evaluation as a means for change, is a process which lasts a lifetime. "The unexamined life is not worth living" is a proverb for the ages. God gave us keen insight and mental acuity to team up with His Holy Spirit in making us the only creatures on the earth capable of this activity. Don't slack up. Remember: *If I am disturbed there is something wrong with me.* Apply the principle to each and every area of distress.

A. Identify the distress: I am afraid, angry, discouraged, etc.

> *Self-examination and personal responsibility are a lifestyle for the one who will live free in Christ. Status quo is not enough. I must be moving forward.*

B. Identify what caused the distress: What was said, what was done, what was thought to prompt this response in me?

C. Identify the aspect of my person which is threatened or offended. Is it my security, my pride, my relationships, etc.?

D. Find what scripture says about the subject.

E. Pray for grace to overcome. Pray for the offending party. Do what the Bible instructs. Claim the promise of God and go forward.

RESTITUTION AND RESTORATION

One of the difficulties we find in walking out our new life is the havoc created by our old one. Every addict and alcoholic has left a trail of destruction behind. We have used people, stolen property, lied for our own profit, and sometimes literally punched people. At the very least, we have abused and shortchanged those who love us by being emotionally inaccessible or unavailable when they needed us most.

God is interested in putting our lives back together. He also wants to see us develop the character required to take responsibility for our own actions. It is woefully insufficient for the "Born Again" addict to announce his conversion and expect everyone he has harmed to see his sins as "under the blood." While God has certainly forgiven us, we still need to make right what we can and soften the blow of our havoc wherever possible. God wants us to be able to walk down the street without shame, unafraid to look anyone in the eye. To this end we must be committed to restitution for what we have taken from others, and to restoration in relationships we have damaged or destroyed.

1. Our God is a God of reconciliation. To reconcile is to restore a friendly relationship or to bring two parties into favor again. This is what God was doing in Christ: He was reconciling the world unto Himself. Read **2 CORINTHIANS 5:17-21**. Notice that the ministry He has given us is the ministry of reconciliation. It is the very nature of God, restoring relationships.

In the following passages, notice the responsibility we have to initiate reconciliation of broken relationships. After reading each passage write what you learn about God's desire to restore, and your role in the process.

MATTHEW 18:15-20 _____

_____

_____

_____

MATTHEW 5:23-26 _____

_____

_____

_____

2. The Bible also teaches the principle of restitution of things taken unlawfully. In order to make ourselves right with our fellows, we must try to balance the books from our old lifestyle. Read the following scriptures and

2 CORINTHIANS 5:18-20
All this newness of life is from God, who brought us back to Himself through what Christ did. And God has given us the task of reconciling people to Him. For God was in Christ, reconciling the world to Himself, no longer counting people's sins against them. This is the wonderful message He has given us to tell others. We are Christ's ambassadors and God is using us to speak to you. We urge you, as though Christ Himself were here pleading with you. "Be reconciled to God."

(New Living Translation)

make a note regarding the principle of restitution:

LEVITICUS 6:1-6 _____

_____

_____

_____

EXODUS 22:1-4 _____

_____

_____

_____

PROVERBS 6:31 _____

_____

_____

LUKE 19:8 _____

_____

_____

PROVERBS 6:31
But if he is caught, he will be fined seven times as much as he stole, even if it means selling everything in his house to pay it back.

(New Living Translation)

It is usually easy to see where we have stolen money or goods. Some thefts are more difficult to recall. How many hours of work did I steal from my employer by coming to work impaired? How much of my family's peace of mind was lost? What damage did I do to the family name? The list could go on. Prayerfully search your heart to think of places where you have robbed others in any way. Using a table like the one below, begin a list to prepare for the process of making it right. Use as much time and paper as you need. Be thorough. You will need to pray and allow the Holy Spirit to bring things to mind. Don't expect to get this done in one sitting.

I stole from:	*I took:*	*I will repay with:*
1. EXAMPLE: My mother	1. Her peace of mind	1. A life of being a blessing
2.	2.	2.
3.	3.	3.

Examine yourself...

3. In addition to repaying debts we have incurred there is also the job of restoring relationships we have damaged. This is not always an easy task and requires real spiritual growth and commitment to Christ. It is not for the fainthearted. The results are always dependent on the response of another, and the doing of it requires the swallowing of pride and the risk of rejection.

If you are serious about living for God and staying genuinely sober, then get ready for an adventure.

If you're serious about living for God and staying genuinely sober, then get ready for an adventure. The results will be gratifying.

There are two general kinds of broken relationships. First, there are those where we have done clear damage through our behavior. We were wrong and need to be forgiven. For this type of restoration the requirement is simple. I must swallow my pride and humbly ask forgiveness. The difficulty lies when my request is denied. I am informed that I am unforgivable. This is when I have the opportunity to really grow, to love and not strike back, to receive my forgiveness from God and allow that to be sufficient.

The second type of broken relationship is where all or part of the fault is on the part of the other person. It may be an abusive parent or an unfaithful spouse. It may be a dishonest business partner. The job for us in this matter is never to lay accusation and blame on the other party. We are living a new life of forgiveness. The task we have is to see where we were wrong, even if it seems to be a small percent in comparison to the wrong done to us. We must make an effort at restoration based on seeking forgiveness for our part, even if that is just the sin of bitterness toward another human. This is difficult for anyone but especially for the addict who is an expert in blaming others. This will often require the help of another believer with whom we can pray and prepare ourselves to do the right thing, to approach the issue with a pure and loving heart without blame and condemnation for the other.

The process here is the same, begin a table with three columns and prayerfully start your list. Remember, the job is to identify your part in the problem, not the other person's.

Examine yourself...

Relationship damaged:	What happened?	My part is:
1. EXAMPLE: my wife	1. She ran off with the kids.	1. I was a lousy husband and father.
2.	2.	2.
3.	3.	3.

4. This process may evoke some difficult emotions. It also may present some interesting dilemmas. What about debts I owe which, if revealed, could lead to my incarceration? What about damage done to relationships, the details of which may be harmful to the other person if they find out? For instance, should I ask forgiveness of a husband whose wife I defiled in an affair, if that husband is ignorant of the offense? Would this not be clearing my conscience at the expense of his pain? These kinds of issues and many others will come up. We have often led complicated lives and unwinding the

twists is not simple. For this purpose, seek the counsel of another believer in whom you have trust. You might consult the list of people with whom you have established accountable relationships.

List three people with whom you might talk over the lists you have made here and seek advice concerning how to proceed.

_____

_____

_____

Now call them until you have made an appointment to discuss these lists. Write your appointment time and place here.

_____

_____

5. Read **ROMANS 12:9-21**. Notice especially verse **18**. Your job is to do as much as lies with you. It's time to do it! In consultation with your confidant, go back over your lists. For each person listed, come up with an action on your part to make restitution or restoration. Write out the list and begin to plan how you will carry out each amend. Begin to carry out the plan as you have opportunity. Stay with the process until you have cleaned the slate to the best of your ability.

Having started the process of cleaning up the debris of your life, you are really on track to live like a Christian. The challenge which now faces you is learning to live in a way which keeps your life free of new damage. The key is to maintain a willingness to admit your own wrongs, in action and in attitude, and remain willing to immediately do what is necessary to set them right. You have begun a life-long journey. Stay the course.

ROMANS 12:18
Do your part to live in peace with everyone, as much as possible.
(New Living Translation)

The practice of inventory, repentance, and restitution is the lifestyle of sobriety.

Learn it now, and learn it well.

COMMITMENT TO SPIRITUAL GROWTH

Read **2 CORINTHIANS 5:17** and **JOHN 3:3-8**. The Bible teaches us that when we place our faith in Christ we are born of the Spirit, or "born again". Our lives begin anew. Just as we were born babies in the flesh we are also born babies in the spirit. We have to go through a process of growing up. We see this throughout scripture. We are encouraged to grow in several areas. God gives us scriptures which describe spiritual babes and children. Just as natural children require food and care, so spiritual babes require feeding and nurture in order to grow. It is important to recognize where we are in our growth and seek those things which help us to grow further. Growing up spiritually is a life-long process and requires a daily commitment on our part.

WHAT IS "SPIRITUAL GROWTH"?

Scripture gives us several characteristics of spiritual babies and children. Read the following passages and write what each one tells you about spiritual childhood. Also note any characteristics of childhood which you can see in yourself.

EPHESIANS 4:14
Then we will no longer be like children, forever changing our minds about what we believe because someone has told us something different or because someone has cleverly lied to us and made the lie sound like the truth.

(New Living Translation)

They are to help us quit being babies, so easily swayed and carried away by every windbag that comes along with some clever gimmick, with some big show to snare the gullible.

(Cotton Patch Translation)

EPHESIANS 4:14 _____
_____
_____
_____

1 CORINTHIANS 3:1-3 _____
_____
_____
_____

HEBREWS 5:11-14 (You might benefit from looking at some other translations of these verses.)
_____
_____
_____
_____
_____

FROM FAITH TO FAITH

The scripture describes three specific areas in which we grow as we continue to walk with Christ. God uses the terms "from.... to...." to describe our movement in these areas: Faith, Strength, and Glory.

Read **ROMANS 1:16-17**. Paul tells us we are to go from faith to faith. One translation says "the way of faith which leads to greater faith." Faith is the means by which we receive all the gifts of God's grace. It enables us to reach out and grasp the promise of God. As we grow in faith we increase our capacity to touch the world by increasing our capacity to believe God for what is needed to get the job done.

1. Look up each of the following scriptures and write what it tells you about faith and how you might grow in it.

ROMANS 10:17 _____

_____

_____

2 THESSALONIANS 1:3 _____

_____

_____

JAMES 1:2-4 _____

_____

_____

2. Notice **HABAKKUK 2:1-4**. Notice the connection between vision and faith. Increasing faith increases our ability to accomplish the vision of God for our lives. Do you have an idea of God's vision for your life? How do you see God using you? What do you see as your gifts and talents? How do your talents, desires, and abilities fit in the church you are attending? Write out a description of what you see in your future as you grow in your faith. Where do you see yourself in one year? In five?

_____

_____

_____

_____

_____

_____

_____

ROMANS 1:16, 17
For I am not ashamed of the gospel of Christ, for it is the power of God to salvation for everyone who believes, for the Jew first and also for the Greek. For in it the righteousness of God is revealed from faith to faith; as it is written, The just shall live by faith.

(New King James)

HABAKKUK 2:2-4
And then God answered, Write this: Write what you see. Write it out in big block letters so that it can be read on the run. This vision – message is a witness pointing to what's coming. It aches for the coming – it can hardly wait! And it doesn't lie. If it seems slow in coming, wait. It's on the way. It will come right on time. Look at that man, bloated by self-importance, full of himself but soul-empty. But the person in right standing before God through loyal and steady believing is fully alive, really alive.

(Message Bible)

...but the just shall live by faith.

(New King James)

FROM STRENGTH TO STRENGTH

PSALM 84:5-7

Blessed is the man whose strength is in You, whose heart is set on pilgrimage. As they pass through the valley of Baca, they make it a spring, the rain also covers it with pools. They go from strength to strength, everyone of them appears before God in Zion.

(New King James)

Read **PSALM 84:5-7**. Notice we are growing from strength to strength and that this occurs as we are determined to walk with God no matter what the circumstance. Strength is the inner fortitude to keep going no matter what happens and to do so with joy. This is made clear in **COLOSSIANS 1:9-11**. Paul prays for the Christians of Colosse. In verse **11**, The Living Bible quotes His prayer like this:

> *"We are praying, too, that you will be filled with his mighty, glorious strength so that you can keep going no matter what happens--always full of the joy of the Lord."*

This precious commodity of strength for the journey comes to us direct from God. It is an impartation by the Spirit to our spirit and can be had by praying for it. It manifests itself most clearly when we are at the end of our own strength and have to call on resources beyond ourselves.

1. Look up the following scriptures on strength and write what you learn about where it comes from and how you get it.

EPHESIANS 6:10 _____

_____

_____

ISAIAH 41:10 _____

_____

_____

ISAIAH 40:29-31 _____

_____

_____

PSALM 138:3

When I pray, you answer me; you encourage me by giving me the strength I need.

(New Living Testament)

The moment I called out, You stepped in, You made my life large with strength.

(Message Bible)

PSALM 138:3 _____

_____

_____

2 TIMOTHY 4:16-18 _____

_____

_____

2 CORINTHIANS 12:9-10 _____

_____

_____

_____

PHILIPPIANS 4:13 _____

_____

_____

_____

PHILIPPIANS 4:13
For I can do everything with the help of Christ who gives me the strength I need.

(New Living Translation)

2. Now take a moment to prayerfully consider your life. What are the challenges you face which are most discouraging and tiring for you? What things are you going through which sometimes tempt you to quit or give up? List these things one by one and pray according to the scriptures above. Ask God specifically for strength to continue in the race.

_____

_____

_____

_____

FROM GLORY TO GLORY

Read **2 CORINTHIANS 3:17-18**. You might want to try several translations. Notice that we are being transformed from glory to glory by the Spirit of the Lord as we look into the mirror of the Word and see Jesus. The idea is that as we get to know Jesus more intimately, we will be changed to be more and more like Him. That is the ultimate goal of Christian growth: to be more like Jesus. This is a process which requires us to look into the Word of God and apply what we learn to our lives. As we do this, the Holy Spirit changes us from the inside out.

1. Look up the following passages and write out what they teach you about the process of becoming more like Jesus.

ROMANS 8:29-31 _____

_____

_____

_____

ROMANS 13:12-14 _____

_____

_____

_____

EPHESIANS 4:22-24 _____

_____

_____

_____

2 CORINTHIANS 3:17-18
Now the Lord is the Spirit: and where the Spirit of the Lord is there is liberty. But we all, with unveiled face beholding as in a mirror the glory of the Lord, are being transformed into the same image from glory to glory as by the Spirit of the Lord.

(New King James)

Now the Lord is the Spirit and wherever the Spirit of the Lord is, He gives freedom. And all us have had the veil removed so that we can be mirrors that brightly reflect the glory of the Lord. And as the Spirit of the Lord works within us, we become more and more like Him and reflect His glory even more.

(New Living Translation)

COLOSSIANS 3:10-16 _____

_____

_____

_____

_____

LUKE 6:40
A student is not greater than the teacher. But the student who works hard will become like the teacher.

(New Living Translation)

LUKE 6:40 _____

_____

_____

_____

2. Now take a moment to prayerfully consider what areas in your life need some special attention. Where are you falling short of a Christ-like life? List each of these areas one by one. Now pray for grace to grow in each area. This is a good time to use your prayer tongue if you have received it. Notice **ROMANS 8:26-27**. The Holy Spirit will help us by praying for our weaknesses in words we cannot understand. Write your list here.

ROMANS 8:26-27
And the Holy Spirit helps us in our distress. For we don't even know what we should pray for, nor how we should pray. But the Holy Spirit prays for us with groanings that cannot be expressed in words. And the Father who knows all hearts knows what the Spirit is saying, for the Spirit pleads for us believers in harmony with God's own will.

(New Living Translation)

_____

_____

_____

_____

_____

ESSENTIALS FOR PROPER SPIRITUAL GROWTH

1. A Commitment to the Process

2. The Word of God

3. Commitment to a Local Church

4. Prayer

Your sobriety is dependent on expanding your spiritual life.

There are several things which are absolutely essential for proper spiritual growth. Leave out any of these ingredients and your growth will be hindered. Like good nutrition, a balanced diet is required to grow in all areas. Remember, your sobriety is dependent on expanding your spiritual life. It is up to you to take responsibility for doing what is necessary to obtain all the ingredients for this. Living on a spiritual plane requires an effort on your part. Take an inventory of yourself in each of the following areas to see where you need to add to your spiritual diet.

This means a day-by-day determination to walk in the path of the spiritual life.

Essential #1:
A Commitment to the Process

The first step in spiritual growth is a commitment to the process. This means a day-by-day determination to walk in the path of the spiritual life. Growing spiritually, getting closer to God, has to become the most important thing in your life. It must be priority. If it is not, it will gradually slip away and become just one more detail to be ignored as you pursue your own interests. It is easy to let this commitment slip as sobriety begins to allow life to return to "normal." Your job, community, family, entertainment, and any of a hundred other good things begin to draw on time and thinking. Spiritual things get pushed aside until they become an afterthought instead of a grand obsession. This is dangerous ground. Renew your commitment to follow God daily.

Read all of **PHILIPPIANS CHAPTER 3**. In this great passage, Paul talks about his own great accomplishments in the natural realm. He gives warnings about certain kinds of people. He then recounts the things which are of real value in his life and reiterates his total commitment to keep growing himself. From this passage, list at least five things you can learn about your commitment to grow spiritually.

_____

_____

_____

_____

_____

Essential #2:
The Word of God

Notice **1 PETER 2:1-3**. Peter tells us that there is more to growing up spiritually than simply ceasing from our sin. While it is important to put away our sinful behavior, real growth only comes when we take in the Word of God like a baby takes in milk. This illustration is meant to show an attitude toward the Word. We are to crave it, demand it, and go to any lengths to get it. Without it, we cannot grow.

One of the most important things the Word of God does in our lives is change the way we think. While we are born of the Spirit, our mind is still cluttered with old thinking and attitudes. Only the application of the Word of God can help us learn to think like spiritual people. Read the following passages and write out what they teach you about the process of changing your thinking.

ROMANS 12:1-3 _____

_____

_____

_____

1 PETER 2:1-3
So get rid of all malicious behavior and deceit. Don't just pretend to be good! Be done with hypocrisy and jealousy and backstabbing. You must crave pure spiritual milk so that you can grow into the fullness of your salvation. Cry out for this nourishment as a baby cries for milk, now that you have had a taste of the Lord's kindness.

(New Living Translation)

So then, sweep your house clean of all meanness and fibbing and double-dealing and green-eyedness and cattiness. Like new babies, yell for the pure Gospel milk that's just right, so that you might get fat and healthy on it. When you got your first taste you saw the Lord is real nourishing.

(Message Bible)

2 CORINTHIANS 10:3-5 _____

_____

_____

_____

JAMES 1:18-25 _____

_____

_____

_____

Review your own relationship to the Bible. How can you change your daily behavior to make more room for spiritual feeding from the Word of God?

_____

_____

_____

Essential #3:
Commitment to a Local Church

The fellowship of other believers is a necessity.

One of the requirements for spiritual growth is consistent ministry from a local fellowship. The Bible teaches that the ministry gifts God has set in the church are required in order to properly prepare Christians for their individual areas of service and to perfect their faith. In addition, the fellowship of other believers is a necessity. We need each other to encourage and correct us. There can be no "lone rangers" in the process of spiritual growth.

Read the description of the function of the five ministries God has set in the Church in **EPHESIANS 4:11-16**. Notice carefully the list of things these gifts are supposed to bring about in our lives. Out of this passage, list four things you see which you are to receive as a result of the five-fold ministry.

_____

_____

_____

_____

Are you in a committed relationship to a local church? If not, why not?

_____

_____

_____

_____

If you are in a good local church and active, thank God. If not, go back to Recovery Principle #3 and review the process of finding a local church. Do it!!

In addition to ministry from the pulpit, we must also have ministry from the pew. Relationship with other believers is important. Without it we can never learn to live out the Kingdom of God. Read each of the following passages and tell what you learn about the necessity of relationships with other Christians.

HEBREWS 10:24-25 _____

_____

_____

_____

PROVERBS 13:20 _____

_____

_____

PROVERBS 27:17 _____

_____

Essential #4:
Prayer

Simply hearing about God from the pulpit, reading about God from the Word, or talking about God with our friends is insufficient to truly know Him. In order to develop relationship with Him we must talk to Him and listen to Him. This activity is called "prayer." A Christian who doesn't pray is an ineffective person. Prayer is the place where we tap into the power of the person of God. Read and comment on each of the following passages.

MATTHEW 26:36-41 _____

_____

_____

_____

LUKE 18:1 _____

_____

_____

_____

ROMANS 12:12 _____

_____

_____

_____

PROVERBS 13:20
Become wise by walking with the wise; Hang out with fools and watch your life fall to pieces.

(Message Bible)

Whoever walks with the wise will become wise; whoever walks with fools will suffer harm.

(New Living Translation)

LUKE 18:1
One day Jesus told His disciples a story to illustrate their need for constant prayer and to show them that they must never give up.

(New Living Translation)

I CORINTHIANS 14:14-15 _____

_____

_____

_____

ROMANS 8:26-27 _____

_____

_____

_____

COLOSSIANS 4:2-4 _____

_____

_____

_____

JAMES 5:16-18
Be honest with one another about your sins and pray for each other that you might get the victory over them, for the petition of a truly good man is powerfully effective. Elijah, for instance, was a human being just like us and he earnestly prayed that it might not rain, and not a drop fell for 3-1/2 years. Then he prayed again and it poured, and things began to grow again.

(Cotton Patch Translation)

JAMES 5:16-18 _____

_____

_____

_____

BELOVED ADDICT, PLEASE REMEMBER THIS!!!!!

Recovery is a process, not an event. It absolutely requires a commitment to ongoing spiritual growth. This means a defined commitment to activities, including church involvement, which enhance and encourage spiritual development. Growing in the spiritual realm must become the primary focus of life or relapse is inevitable.

SERVICE TO OTHERS

The purpose of God in saving you from yourself was much greater than simply allowing you to live. It goes beyond even the blessing of those who love you. It extends to actually using your life to bring service to others. Perhaps the greatest truth of sobriety is that *our lives now have purpose*. Unless we allow ourselves to fulfill this purpose, we will thwart the desire of God to give us a life which is satisfying and useful.

1. The Lord Jesus Christ came to give His life in service to others. Though He was, in fact, God and could have demanded obedience and worship, He gave Himself to save people. He has left this for us as an example of a godly attitude. In each of the following passages comment on what lessons you can learn from Jesus and His example.

MARK 10:42-45
Jesus got them together to settle things down. "You've observed how godless rulers throw their weight around," He said, "and when people get a little power how quickly it goes to their heads. It's not going to be that way with you. Whoever wants to be first among you must be your slave. This is what the Son of Man has done: He came to serve, not to be served – and then to give away His life in exchange for many who are held hostage."

(Message Bible)

MARK 10:42-45 _____
_____
_____
_____
_____

LUKE 22:24-30 _____
_____
_____
_____
_____

JOHN 13:1-17 _____
_____
_____
_____

PHILIPPIANS 2:5-16 _____
_____
_____
_____
_____

2. Every person who comes into the Kingdom of God has a pre-planned purpose in life. We are created to serve one another. When we fail to enter into our service we are frustrated and often irritable. Many live an unhappy sobriety and some eventually slide back into addiction because they fail to enter

the joyful world of service to others. Read each of the following passages and comment on what they teach you about service to others and God's purposes for you. Look these verses up in several different translations, if possible.

EPHESIANS 2:8-10 _____

_____
_____
_____

GALATIANS 5:13-15 _____

_____
_____

1 PETER 4:10-11 _____

_____
_____

MATTHEW 5:13-16 _____

_____
_____
_____

MATTHEW 25:35-40 _____

_____
_____

> **GALATIANS 5:13-15**
> *It is absolutely clear that God has called you to a free life. Just make sure that you don't use this freedom as an excuse to do whatever you want to do and destroy your freedom. Rather, use your freedom to serve one another in love; that's how freedom grows. For everything we know about God's Word is summed up in a single sentence: Love others as you love yourself. That's an act of true freedom.*
>
> (Message Bible)

3. There is a great secret which is key to understanding life in the Spirit: You can't keep what you don't give away. Giving and receiving is the rhythm of the Kingdom of God. When we grasp this principle and begin to apply it in every area of our lives, we soon see wonderful results. If sobriety is dear to you, give the gift to another and you will multiply your joy. If salvation is precious to you, increase your grace by giving the gift to one who is lost. This is the way we live. Comment on each of the following passages.

ACTS 20:35 _____

_____
_____
_____

PSALM 41:1-3 _____

_____
_____
_____

> **PSALM 41:1-3**
> *Oh the joys of those who are kind to the poor. The Lord rescues them in times of trouble. The Lord protects them and keeps them alive. He gives them prosperity and rescues them from their enemies. The Lord nurses them when they are sick and eases their pain and discomfort.*
>
> (New Living Translation)

PSALM 112:5-9 _____

_____

_____

_____

2 CORINTHIANS 9:6-12 _____

_____

_____

_____

PHILIPPIANS 4:17-20 _____

_____

_____

_____

GALATIANS 6:6-10 _____

_____

_____

_____

LUKE 6:31-38 _____

_____

_____

_____

EPHESIANS 5:1,2
Watch what God does, and then you do it, like children who learn proper behavior from their parents. Mostly what God does is love you. Keep company with Him and learn a life of love. Observe how Christ loved us. His love was not cautious but extravagant. He didn't love in order to get something from us but to give everything of Himself to us. Love like that.

(Message Bible)

4. When we come to Christ we become new creatures. Our hearts are changed and we are created in the image of our Father. He is the ultimate giver. It is our nature to give, to love, to serve. It is the theme of our existence. It is the reason we pray, the reason we work, the reason God prospers us: to be a blessing. Our job is simply to learn who God has made us and be that.

Read **EPHESIANS 5:1-2** in some translation other than the King James. Notice, we are to follow God as our example in love. The way we do this is by imitating Christ. What a calling! We are children of God, having His very own nature. All we must do is imitate our Dad!

5. Read **ROMANS 12:1-8**. Notice the process here. We come to God and offer our bodies to him as a sacrifice. We then go to the Word of God to learn to think like Him. We humble ourselves to serve wherever necessary. We recognize that we are part of a Body and that we will all have different gifts and abilities. The job is to recognize our gifts and use them to serve the Body.

Every Christian has gifts and abilities given by God to use to bless others (**1 PETER 4:10**). That includes you. You are gifted by God. The question is, what are your gifts?

Read **2 CORINTHIANS 1:3-4**. This tells us that each of us is especially equipped to help those who have been in the same kinds of trials that we have. This is why addicts are especially gifted to help addicts, abused women to help other abused women, and so forth. This is a spiritual principle. You can always be a blessing just by sharing your strength with one who is enduring the same trial which you have overcome. Make a list of trials you have come through with God's help. These are guideposts to areas where you may be of service.

_____
_____
_____
_____
_____

6. The Scripture tells us that we are all to give of our finances. **EPHESIANS 4:28** says our jobs are for the purpose of having money to give. Giving is ordained of God and He has given us three basic areas in which we can give. 10% (the tithe) of our income goes to the local church to finance the operations and outreaches available there. We also are asked to give offerings above the tithe for special projects in and out of our local church. As Christians, we will also occasionally give alms. Alms are gifts given to the poor to provide for their need. These are given by individuals to individuals as the compassion of God leads. Read the following scriptures. What do they tell you about giving?

MALACHI 3:8-12 _____
_____
_____
_____

PROVERBS 3:9-10 _____
_____
_____

2 CORINTHIANS 9:6-11 _____
_____
_____

PROVERBS 19:17 _____
_____
_____
_____

2 CORINTHIANS 1:3-4

...He comes alongside us when we go through hard times, and before you know it, He brings us alongside someone else who is going through hard times so that we can be there for that person just as God was there for us.

(Message Bible)

...He is the source of every mercy and the God who comforts us. He comforts us in all our troubles so that we can comfort others. When others are troubled, we will be able to give them the same comfort God has given us.

(New Living Translation)

PROVERBS 3:9-10
Honor the Lord with your wealth and with the best part of everything your land produces. Then He will fill your barns with grain and your vats will overflow with wine.

(New Living Translation)

Honor God with everything you own: give Him the first and the best. Your barns will burst, your wine vats will brim over.

(Message Bible)

MATTHEW 6:1-4 _____

_____
_____
_____

7. In addition to our personal experiences and our finances, we each have gifts and talents given supernaturally by God. We all have them and they are important to God. Every person is a gift to the Body of Christ and his abilities are necessary. We must each find our gifts and use them. Read **1 CORINTHIANS 12:12-27** and tell what you see in this passage.

_____
_____
_____
_____
_____
_____
_____

Often our gifts show up in what we are good at. Make a list of things you are good at. This might range from talking to people, to throwing parties, to working on cars, to teaching kids, or anything where you have had some success in your life.

_____
_____
_____
_____

ACTS 7:23
But when he was 40 years old, it came into his heart to visit his brothers, the children of Israel.
(New King James)

When he was about 40, it was laid on his heart to investigate the conditions of his own Jewish people.
(Cotton Patch Translation)

Another way our gifts show up is by what is in our heart. What do you really enjoy or have a desire to do? Often God guides us by placing desires in our heart. Notice how He led Moses in **ACTS 7:23**. What is in your heart? Are there certain kinds of people or ministries which particularly touch your emotions? All these things may be signs of where God wants to use you in some way. Make a list of the things you enjoy and the things which are particularly dear to your heart.

_____
_____
_____
_____
_____

Another way we learn our gifts is by asking others who know us. Sit down with at least two people who know you and ask them what they think you are good at. What do they see as your real assets and gifts? List their responses here.

_____

_____

_____

_____

From the information you have gathered, make a list of at least three things you think may be areas where you are gifted or where God wants to use you.

_____

_____

_____

_____

Now make an appointment with your pastor or the person in your church responsible for volunteer services. Take your list to them and discuss it. Make yourself available to serve in any way, with an eye to using your gifts and following the desires of your heart. Plan to be faithful in your duties. Don't be surprised at what God does with you as you are faithful over the gifts He has given you.

Remember: All the flowers of tomorrow are in the seeds of today.

CONCLUSION

Alcoholism, addiction and other life-controlling habits destroy their victims in a most unkind way. They first destroy all that is lovely, then all that is loved. Their victims become pariahs, shunned and shamed until they are isolated, miserable, and despised. The good news is that addicts and their families are being restored to more than normal well-being every day through the grace of God. The only thing necessary is the courage to make a beginning. Once that decision is made, the only way to lose is to quit. My heroes are those who have stayed the course and walked their way back to useful living. That can be you. It doesn't matter where you fell from or where you dropped to, there is life after addiction. I'll share with you the verses which so helped me when I started the process of recovery on March 4, 1979.

> **PSALM 116:1-6**
> *I love the Lord because He has heard my voice and my*
> *supplications. Because He has inclined His ear to me,*
> *therefore I will call upon Him as long as I live. The pains of*
> *death encompassed me, and the pains of hell laid hold of me:*
> *I found trouble and sorrow. Then I called upon the name of*
> *the Lord; O Lord, I implore You, deliver my soul. Gracious*
> *is the Lord, and righteous; yes, our God is merciful. The Lord*
> *preserves the simple: I was brought low, and He saved me.*
>
> (New King James)

He will help you, too, and we are committed to *"Building People of Substance for Works of Power."* If we may help you in your quest to become a person of substance, contact our offices. Keep the faith, keep your heart, and keep in touch.

Pastor Virgil L. Stokes

APPENDIX

SUGGESTED READING

1. *Alcoholics Anonymous* (The Big Book) Third Edition (Alcoholics Anonymous World Services, Inc., New York, 1976.

2. *Serenity, A Companion for 12 Step Recovery*, Thomas Nelson Publishers.

3. *The Basic Text*, Narcotics Anonymous.

4. *Gamblers Anonymous - Sharing Recovery Through Gamblers Anonymous* (ISBN 0-917839-00-5).

5. *Gamblers Anonymous - A New Beginning.*

6. Joe McQueen, *The Steps We Took.*

7. Melodie Beattie, *Codependent No More: How to Stop Controlling Others and Start Caring for Yourself.*

8. *The 12 Steps-A Spiritual Journey* (a working guide to healing damaged emotions) [ISBN 0-941405-44-3].

9. *The 12 Steps for Christians* [ISBN 0-941405-57-5].

10. *Prayers for the 12 Steps-A Spiritual Journey* [ISBN 0-941405-28-1].

11. *The Life Recovery Bible*, [ISBN 0-8423-2809-2] (excellent for anyone in recovery).

12. *Living Free* (a guide to forming recovery ministries, written for pastors and church leaders) [ISBN 0-941405-16-8].

13. *The 12 Steps--A Way Out* (Focuses on issues common to people raised in troubled homes) [ISBN 0-941405-11-7].

14. *The 12 Steps for Adult Children* [ISBN 0-941405-08-7].

15. *Overeaters Anonymous – OA.*

16. William Backus & Marie Chapian, *Telling Yourself the Truth.*

17. Paul Meier, M.D., *Don't Let Jerks Get the Best of You* (Thomas Nelson Publishers, Nashville).

18. Frank Minirth & Paul Meier, *Happiness is a Choice.*

19. Frank Minirth, et al, *Love Hunger.*

20. Vernon E. Johnson, *I'll Quit Tomorrow* [ISBN 0-06-250430-4].

21. Anderson Spickard, M.D. & Barbara R. Thompson, *Dying for a Drink.*

22. Robert S. McGee, *The Search for Significance* (Rapha Publishing, Houston) [ISBN 0- 945276-07-9].

23. Pat Springle, *Codependency.*

24. McGee, Springle, & Joiner, *Rapha's 12-Step Program for Overcoming Chemical Dependency.*

THE TWELVE STEPS
OF ALCOHOLICS ANONYMOUS

1. We admitted that we were powerless over alcohol - that our lives had become unmanageable.

2. Came to believe that a Power greater than ourselves could restore us to sanity.

3. Made a decision to turn our will and our lives over to the care of God as we understood Him.

4. Made a searching and fearless moral inventory of ourselves.

5. Admitted to God, to ourselves, and to another human being the exact nature of our wrongs.

6. Became entirely ready to have God remove all these defects of character.

7. Humbly asked Him to remove our shortcomings.

8. Made a list of all persons we had harmed and became willing to make amends to them all.

9. Made direct amends to such people whenever possible, except when to do so would injure them or others.

10. Continued to take personal inventory and when we were wrong promptly admitted it.

11. Sought through prayer and meditation to improve our conscious contact with God as we understood Him, praying only for the knowledge of His will for us and the power to carry that out.

12. Having had a spiritual awakening as the result of these steps, we tried to carry this message to alcoholics, and to practice these principles in all our affairs.

SEVEN PRINCIPLES OF RECOVERY

The following are principles necessary to the recovery of any addict:

1. Deflation: Admission - Desperation - Willingness

    Admission: This is the destruction of the alibi system, a breakdown of denial.

    Desperation: This is the end of hope in self-effort and ability.

    Willingness: The motivation to take difficult action which comes from the awareness that there are no alternatives or compromises.

2. Faith in God: Dependence on God, not self. Prayer and Bible Study.

3. Accountability: Development of internal controls

4. Self-examination

5. Restitution and restoration: Without these steps repentance is a mental exercise, not a spiritual reality.

6. Committed to ongoing spiritual growth: Church!

7. Service to others.

ABOUT THE AUTHOR
VIRGIL L. STOKES

Rev. Virgil L. Stokes is a graduate of the University of Oklahoma and worked for several years as a Registered Nurse in the mental health field. He is experienced in working with troubled adolescents, the mentally ill, and the chemically dependent. Having personally experienced the ravages of alcoholism, as a recovered alcoholic/addict, and the power of God to deliver, he brings special insight and revelation to this much-debated issue.

Virgil, and his wife Judy, have been in ministry since 1980. They have served four churches as pastors. They are both graduates of Rhema Bible Training Center and are ordained by Faith Christian Fellowship, International, for whom they serve as field representatives. From 1985 until 1995 they served as pastors of Living Water Faith Fellowship in Oneonta, NY before moving to Arizona. They are now pastors of Faith Christian Fellowship of Tucson, Arizona.

The Stokeses are founders of Abundant Heart Ministries, a missionary/evangelistic association involved in training pastors and church leaders at home and abroad. They also founded Faith Ministry Training Institute in Tucson, Arizona. Training programs now exist in Mexico, Panama, and on Indian Reservations in the United States. Abundant Heart's schools are designed to move Christians from the pew into the Harvest. In addition, the Stokeses write and publish printed materials in English and Spanish, especially designed to help ministers become more effective.

Rev. Stokes is deeply committed to strengthening local churches. He sees the local church as the key element in God's plan for reaching the world and is committed to encouraging the church to partake of the supernatural power deposited in her through the Holy Spirit while remaining faithful to the revealed truth of God's Word.

Faith Christian Fellowship of Tucson

P.O. Box 89156 • Tucson, AZ 85752

Phone: (520) 792-3238

E-mail: virgil@fcftucson.org • Web Site: www.fcftucson.org

LaVergne, TN USA
22 February 2011

217389LV00008BC/1/P